Instructor's Manual

to accompany

Music First!
THIRD EDITION

Gary White
Iowa State University

Boston, Massachusetts   Burr Ridge, Illinois   Dubuque, Iowa
Madison, Wisconsin   New York, New York   San Francisco, California   St. Louis, Missouri

McGraw-Hill

A Division of The McGraw·Hill Companies

Cover illustration by Russ Willms

ISBN 0-697-29382-3

Printed in the United States of America

10 9 8 7 6 5 4

Contents

Introduction

Music First! is an introduction to the fundamentals of music for students who are just beginning their formal music education. The premise of the book is that intellectual understanding of music should grow out of direct experience—that *music* should come *first!* Thus, the study of fundamentals is combined with considerable experience in music reading to enable students to begin making music. Other forms of musical involvement such as listening, composing, and some formal ear training are provided in the text, and you can select from these musical experiences according to the level of the class and your own preferences.

The primary performance media are the voice and the keyboard, but provisions are made for guitar and other instruments. With the availability of portable electronic keyboards, the application of the fundamentals to a keyboard setting is becoming more and more important. A brief introduction to MIDI keyboards and their use with the *Personal Tutor* software is included in appendix 3 on page 160 of the text. Students with background in guitar, recorder, or other instruments may wish to use those instruments in class participation.

This course is designed so that students will develop more than an intellectual understanding of the fundamentals of music. You are encouraged to be inventive in devising appropriate activities for your students.

The cassette provides the musical background for the student's introduction to rhythm and pitch. It may be used individually and in class in the early chapters. It is important, however, that the student develop a strong internal sense of pulse, so the cassette should be phased out gradually and replaced by clapping, tapping, or conducting the beat.

Providing suitable music for individual and class participation is critical to this broad-based approach to music learning. The songbook beginning on page 183 in the text includes over seventy songs with popular music chord symbols and guitar tablatures. The songs represent a cross section of musical styles and, for the most part, are familiar to students and teachers. All of the songs are also recorded on the cassettes. These recordings are referred to in the listening sections in each chapter, and they can also be used as a background for the students' performances.

The level of student performance will vary greatly, and it is important to remember that performance is intended as an adjunct to the study of fundamentals rather than an end in itself. Thus, the natural tendency of musicians to rehearse and perfect their performance may not be appropriate in the music fundamentals classroom.

A wide variety of written activities and assignments is included to assist in the development of intellectual understanding. These materials may be worked out as part of the written preparation for the course, used as class activities, or collected for evaluation purposes. Many of the early concepts require considerable drill and practice to achieve fluency, and I have provided considerable variety in materials. Written work is absolutely essential to success in teaching the fundamentals of music. The activities of the class should be centered on developing accuracy and fluency with the materials of music.

Since a music fundamentals course is often considered to be a part of the "general education" curriculum, I have included a number of "Interludes," which encourage thought and discussion about a broad range of musical topics.

In summary, it is my opinion that a well-balanced fundamentals of music course should include written activities, singing, instrumental performance, listening, verbal response, and discussion so that the fundamentals are fully assimilated.

The third edition of *Music First!* features three significant changes:

1.   The *Personal Tutor* software is available in the computer version of *Music First!* This Macintosh™ software is on a single 800k disk that is packaged with the book. The software runs from this disk and should not be copied to a hard drive, since it is initialized for each individual student and a record of the student's progress is maintained on the disk. Instructions for working with the software are included at the end of each chapter of the book and in appendix 3 on page 160 of the text. (Further instructions for using the software can be found later in this introduction.)

2.   Exercises have been added at the end of most chapters to encourage students to identify the musical elements they are learning in music that is familiar to them. After all, the ultimate goal of the study of fundamentals is the ability to apply this knowledge to music performance or appreciation. Music already known to the student is an ideal place to begin this process.

3.   The songbook, which was a separate item in previous editions, is now bound into the book itself.

Course Plans

The text is intended for a one-semester course but it could be used for a one-quarter course by eliminating the final chapters. A two-quarter sequence would be ideal and would allow all the materials to be fully developed even with students having no musical background. A two-semester integrated sequence can be devised by: following *Music First!* with a beginning class piano method such as Starr/Starr, *Practical Piano Skills* (Brown & Benchmark), to provide a keyboard emphasis; combining the text with a sightsinging manual such as Benward/ Carr, *Sightsinging Complete* (Brown & Benchmark), to provide a music reading emphasis; combining the book with a listening text such as Ferris, *Music, The Art of Listening* (Brown & Benchmark), to provide a listening emphasis; or following the book with a general humanities text such as Lamm, *The Search for Personal Freedom*, to provide a humanities emphasis. *Music First!* was designed for a one-semester, two-credit music fundamentals course at Iowa State University, where it has been extensively class tested for over eight years.

The following course plans will provide a starting point for developing your syllabus. The musical background of the students must be considered in planning the course, so two alternate plans are included, one assuming little or no musical background and one assuming some experience with reading music but no formal theory instruction.

Semester Plan—assuming no musical training

Week	Chapter	Content
1	1	Rhythmic notation, simple and compound division
2	2	Notation of pitch, introduction to reading pitch notation
3	3	Simple meter, development of reading rhythmic notation
4	3	and combining rhythm and pitch reading
5	4	Compound meter
6	5	Accidentals, development of whole and half steps, reading key signatures
7	6	Major scales/keys, concept of tonic and dominant, solfeggio, circle of fifths,
8	6	singing rounds
9	7	Intervals
10	7	"
11	8	Minor scales/keys, relative and parallel relationships
12	8	"
13	9	Chords, popular music chord symbols
14	9	"
15	10	Harmony, primary chords, roman numeral analysis, harmonic progression
16	10	"

(This course plan omits Chapter 11.)

Semester Plan—assuming musical training but no theory background

Week	Chapter	Content
1	1-2	Rhythmic and pitch notation, simple and compound division, music reading
2	3	Simple meter, development of reading rhythmic notation
3	3	and combining rhythm and pitch reading
4	4	Compound meter
5	5	Accidentals, development of whole and half steps, reading key signatures
6	6	Major scales/keys, concept of tonic and dominant, solfeggio, circle of fifths,
7	6	singing rounds
8	7	Intervals
9	7	"
10	8	Minor scales/keys, relative and parallel relationships
11	8	"
12	9	Chords, popular music chord symbols
13	9	"
14	10	Harmony, primary chords, roman numeral analysis, harmonic progression
15	10-11	Harmonizing melodies, work on creative projects
16	11	Creative projects

Quarter Plan—assuming no musical training

Week	Chapter	Content
1	1	Rhythmic notation, simple and compound division
2	2	Notation of pitch, introduction to reading pitch notation
3	3	Simple meter, development of reading rhythmic notation
4	3	and combining rhythm and pitch reading
5	4	Compound meter
6	5	Accidentals, development of whole and half steps, reading key signatures
7	6	Major scales/keys, concept of tonic and dominant, solfeggio, circle of fifths,
8	6	singing rounds
9	7	Intervals
10	7	"
11	8	Minor scales/keys, relative and parallel relationships
12	8	"

(This plan omits chapters 9-11.)

Quarter Plan—assuming musical training but no theory background

Week	Chapter	Content
1	1-2	Rhythmic and pitch notation, simple and compound division, music reading
2	3	Simple meter, development of reading rhythmic notation
3	3	and combining rhythm and pitch reading
4	4	Compound meter
5	5	Accidentals, development of whole and half steps, reading key signatures
6	6	Major scales/keys, concept of tonic and dominant, solfeggio, circle of fifths,
7	6	singing rounds
8	7	Intervals
9	7	"
10	8	Minor scales/keys, relative and parallel relationships
11	8	"
12	9	Chords, popular music chord symbols

(This plan omits chapters 10-11. If the musical background of the students is quite strong, consider compressing weeks 2-3 into a single week and weeks 5-11 into five weeks to allow for the inclusion of chapters 10 and 11.)

Testing

Regular study habits are a must for success in learning the fundamentals, and I have found that quizzes over each chapter are superior to periodic hour exams. The quizzes included in this *Instructor's Manual* provide samples of class-tested quizzes. They may be administered in a few minutes of class time, often requiring no more than five minutes to complete.

A second component of the testing program is homework. I suggest that you collect and grade a representative sample of the homework assignments.

A third part of evaluation should be testing of skills. If you emphasize ear training, listening, keyboard, or singing you should test these skills.

A multiple-choice final examination (in two forms) that may be machine-scored is included in the *Instructor's Manual*. These examinations have been class tested and analyzed to improve discrimination and reliability.

All test materials may be reproduced without permission from the publisher when they are used with *Music First!*

Teaching Aids

Constant drill and practice is essential for successful learning of the fundamentals. A package of overhead projector transparency masters is included with the *Instructor's Manual*. More class time can be devoted to teaching if your illustration materials have been prepared in advance on overhead transparencies. In addition, you can use the exercises contained within the chapters for in-class practice.

The cassettes are also useful teaching aids. The exercises to accompany beginning music reading experiences are particularly useful in the class setting since they free you to join with the students (or provide individual help) while the tape leads the activity.

Using the *Personal Tutor* Software

When the student first launches the *Personal Tutor* the software asks for the student's name. When the student responds, the program stores an invisible file on the disk with the student's name and a record of the student's success on each of the modules. This file must be present for the student to be recognized and given problems appropriate to his/her level. If it becomes necessary to transfer the software to a new disk due to damage of the original disk it is important that the copy be made by moving the original disk icon to the new disk icon. If you simply copy the *Personal Tutor* application to a new disk the student's record will be lost.

A new *Personal Tutor* disk can be created by copying the visible files to a new disk. When the software is launched from the new disk it will go through the initialization process described above.

The *Personal Tutor* software can be copied without permission from the publisher when it is used with *Music First!*

Chapter Quizzes

QUIZ-Chapter 1a-Rhythm

Name_____

Add up the number of quarter note beats in each pattern and select the correct answer from the five choices given. Place your answer in the blank at the right.

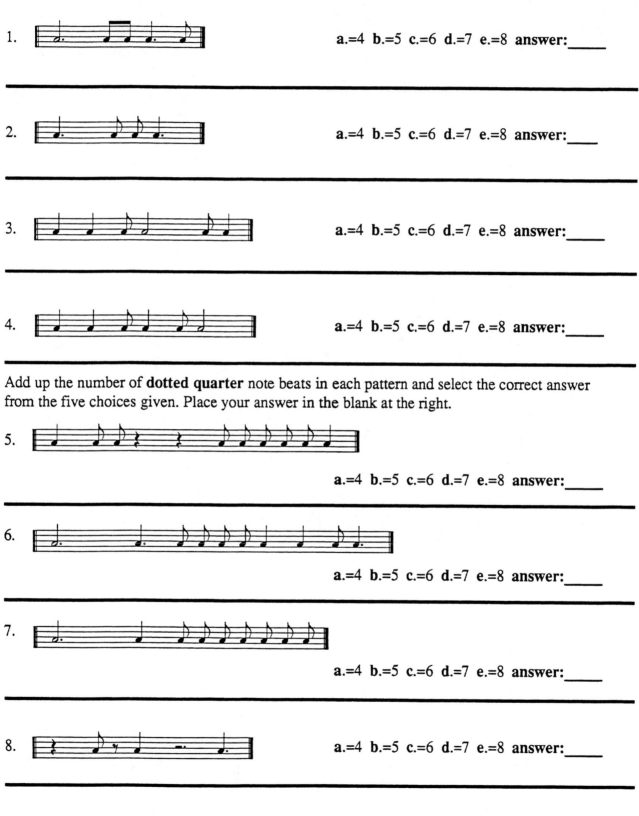

1. **a.=4 b.=5 c.=6 d.=7 e.=8 answer:____**

2. **a.=4 b.=5 c.=6 d.=7 e.=8 answer:___**

3. **a.=4 b.=5 c.=6 d.=7 e.=8 answer:____**

4. **a.=4 b.=5 c.=6 d.=7 e.=8 answer:____**

Add up the number of **dotted quarter** note beats in each pattern and select the correct answer from the five choices given. Place your answer in the blank at the right.

5. **a.=4 b.=5 c.=6 d.=7 e.=8 answer:____**

6. **a.=4 b.=5 c.=6 d.=7 e.=8 answer:____**

7. **a.=4 b.=5 c.=6 d.=7 e.=8 answer:____**

8. **a.=4 b.=5 c.=6 d.=7 e.=8 answer:____**

9. Define the following terms:

Stem:

Flag:

Beam:

Dot:

10. Write examples of the following musical symbols:

Dotted half note:

Eighth rest:

Two quarter notes with tie:

Pair of eighth notes with beam:

QUIZ-Chapter 1b-Rhythm

Name_____

Add up the number of quarter note beats in each pattern and select the correct answer from the five choices given. Place your answer in the blank at the right.

1 a.=4 b.=5 c.=6 d.=7 e.=8 answer:____

2. a.=4 b.=5 c.=6 d.=7 e.=8 answer:____

3. a.=4 b.=5 c.=6 d.=7 e.=8 answer:____

4. a.=4 b.=5 c.=6 d.=7 e.=8 answer:____

Add up the number of **dotted quarter** note beats in each pattern and select the correct answer from the five choices given. Place your answer in the blank at the right.

5. a.=4 b.=5 c.=6 d.=7 e.=8 answer:____

6. a.=4 b.=5 c.=6 d.=7 e.=8 answer:____

7. a.=4 b.=5 c.=6 d.=7 e.=8 answer:____

8. a.=4 b.=5 c.=6 d.=7 e.=8 answer:____

9. Define the following terms:

Rest:

Tie:

Beat:

Flag:

10. Write examples of the following musical symbols:

Single eighth note:

Dotted half note:

Quarter rest:

Two half notes with tie:

QUIZ-Chapter 1c-Rhythm

Name_____

For each note given below, draw the equivalent rest (see example).

Ex.

1.

2.

For each rest given below, draw the equivalent note.

3.

4.

5.

6.   Define the following terms:

Notehead:

Beam:

Repeat signs:

Tempo:

Simple division:

Name_____

For each note given below draw the equivalent rest (see example).

Ex.

1.

2.

For each rest given below draw the equivalent note.

3.

4.

5.

6. Define the following terms:

Beat:

Flag:

Dot:

Compound division:

Rhythmic pattern:

QUIZ-Chapter 2a-Pitch

Name_____

1. Draw the clef indicated and write the note:

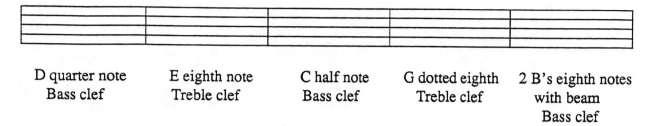

D quarter note	E eighth note	C half note	G dotted eighth	2 B's eighth notes
Bass clef	Treble clef	Bass clef	Treble clef	with beam
				Bass clef

2. Name the given notes (A, B, C, D, E, F, G) on the blanks below:

___ ___ ___ ___ ___ ___ ___ ___ ___ ___

3. Define the following terms:

Middle C:

Ledger line:

Grand staff:

Slur:

4. Write a note an octave above or below the given notes as indicated:

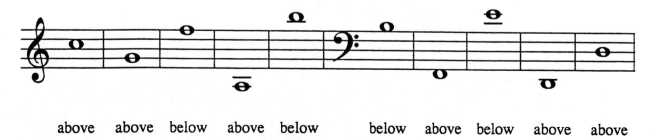

above   above   below   above   below   below   above   below   above   above

QUIZ-Chapter 2b-Pitch

Name_____

1. Draw the clef indicated and write the note:

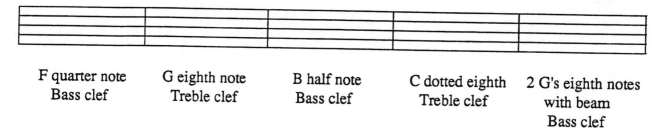

F quarter note	G eighth note	B half note	C dotted eighth	2 G's eighth notes
Bass clef	Treble clef	Bass clef	Treble clef	with beam
				Bass clef

2. Name the given notes (A, B, C, D, E, F, G) on the blanks below:

___ ___ ___ ___ ___ ___ ___ ___ ___ ___

3. Define the following terms:

Clef:

Octave:

Staff:

Grand Staff:

4. Write a note an octave above or below the given notes as indicated:

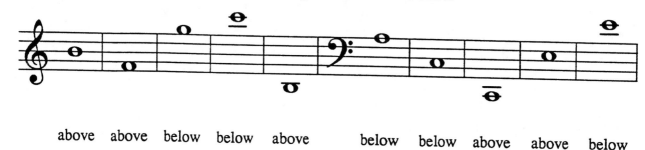

above   above   below   below   above   below   below   above   above   below

Name_____

1. Draw the clef indicated and write the note:

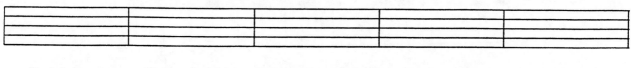

F eighth note	F quarter note	D dotted half note	G dotted eighth note	C whole note
Treble clef	Bass clef	Treble Clef	Bass clef	Treble clef

2. Name the given notes (A, B, C, D, E, F, G) on the blank below:

____ ____ ____ ____ ____ ____ ____ ____

3. Define the following terms:

Pitch:

Treble clef:

Octave:

Staff:

4. Mark the following notes on the keyboard:

1. B

2. C

3. G

4. F

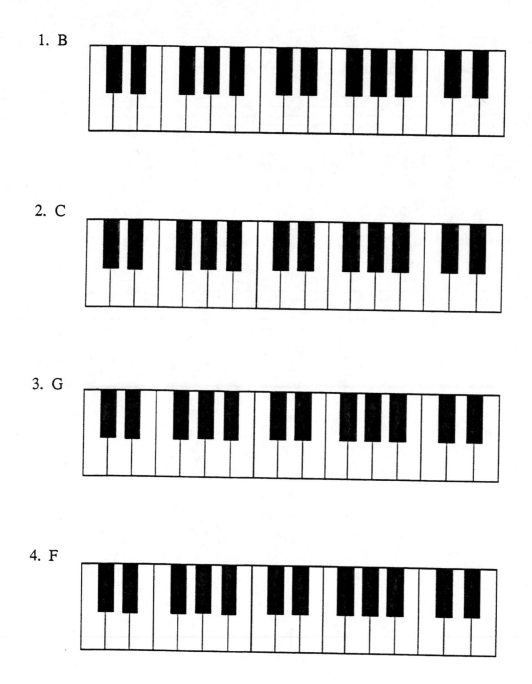

Name_____

1. Draw the clef indicated and write the note:

E two eighth notes with beam Treble clef
A dotted half note Bass clef
D dotted quarter quarter note Treble Clef
C whole note Bass clef
F two eighth notes with beam Treble clef

2. Name the given notes (A, B, C, D, E, F, G) on the blank below:

___ ___ ___ ___ ___ ___ ___ ___

3. Define the following terms:

Slur:

Bass clef:

Middle C:

Ledger line:

4. Mark the following notes on the keyboard:

1. A

2. E

3. C

4. D

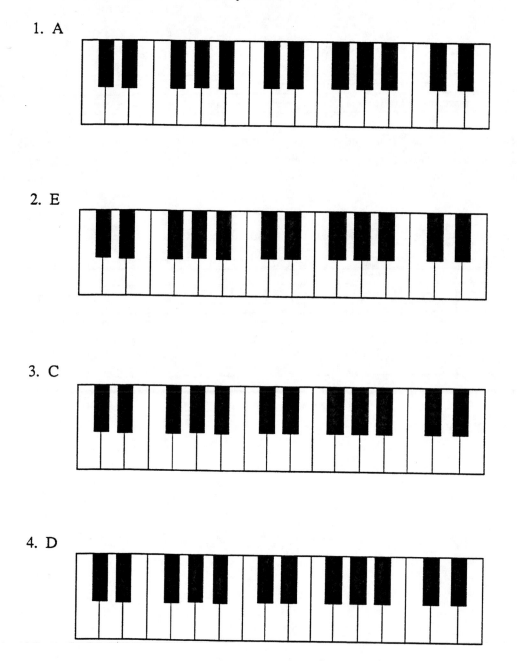

Name_____

Determine the proper meter signature for each of the following rhythms. Place your answer in the blank at the right. (There may be more than one correct answer.)

1.   answer:____

2.   answer:____

3.   answer:____

4.   answer:____

5. Give the note value for the beat and the division of the beat for each of the following meter signatures (**Draw the note and give its name**):

Meter signature: Note value for beat: Note value for division of beat:

$\frac{3}{4}$ _ _ _ _ _ _ _   _ _ _ _ _ _ _ _ _ _

$\frac{2}{8}$ _ _ _ _ _ _ _   _ _ _ _ _ _ _ _ _ _

$\frac{4}{2}$ _ _ _ _ _ _ _   _ _ _ _ _ _ _ _ _ _

$\frac{2}{4}$ _ _ _ _ _ _ _   _ _ _ _ _ _ _ _ _ _

6. Define: Accent

Name_____

Determine the proper meter signature for each of the following rhythms. Place your answer in the blank at the right. (There may be more than one correct answer.)

1.   answer:_____

2.   answer:_____

3.   answer:_____

4.   answer:_____

5. Give the note value for the beat and the division of the beat for each of the following meter signatures (**Draw the note and give its name**):

Meter signature: Note value for beat: Note value for division of beat:

2
4   – – – – – – –   – – – – – – – – –

3
8   – – – – – – –   – – – – – – – – –

4
2   – – – – – – –   – – – – – – – – –

3
4   – – – – – – –   – – – – – – – – –

6.   Define: Measure

Determine the proper meter signature for each of the following rhythms. Place your answer in the blank at the right. (There may be more than one correct answer.)

1.   **answer:_____**

2.   **answer:_____**

3.   **answer:_____**

4.   **answer:_____**

Create two measures of music for the following meter signatures. The first measure should contain note values corresponding to the beat and the second measure should contain note values corresponding to the divisions of the beat. (See the example which follows.)

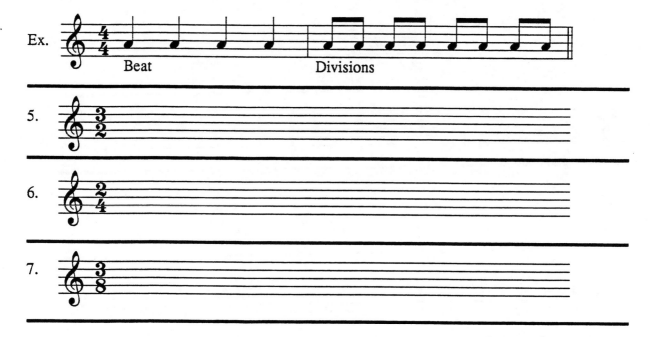

Ex.   Beat   Divisions

5.

6.

7.

8.   Define: Upbeat

Name_____

Determine the proper meter signature for each of the following rhythms. Place your answer in the blank at the right. (There may be more than one correct answer.)

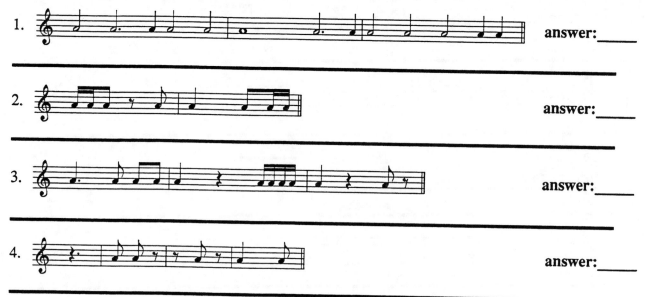

1.   answer:_____

2.   answer:_____

3.   answer:_____

4.   answer:_____

Create two measures of music for the following meter signatures. The first measure should contain note values corresponding to the beat and the second measure should contain note values corresponding to the divisions of the beat. (See the example which follows.)

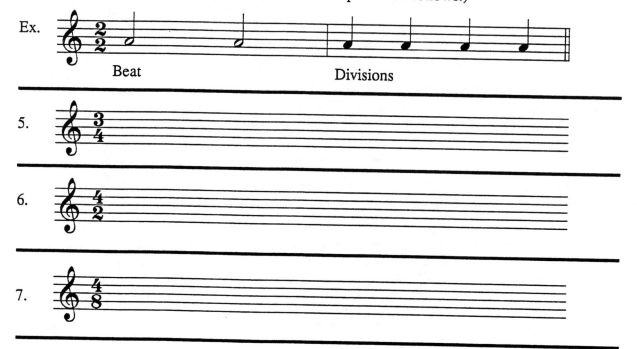

Ex.

Beat   Divisions

5. $\frac{3}{4}$

6. $\frac{4}{2}$

7. $\frac{4}{8}$

8.   Define: Cut time

Name_____

Determine the proper meter signature for each of the following rhythms. Place your answer in the blank at the right.

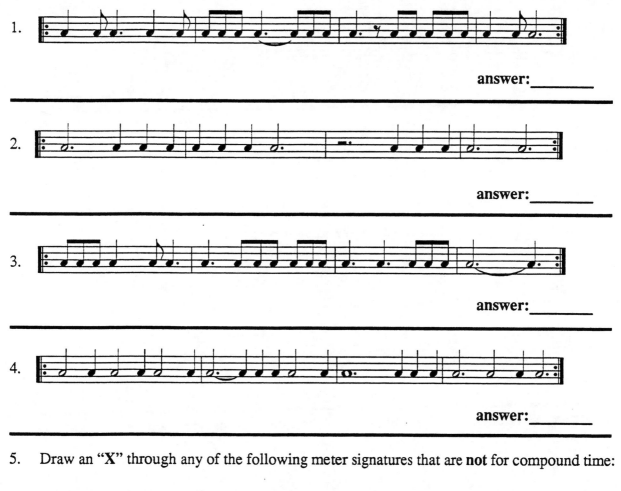

1.

answer:_____

2.

answer:_____

3.

answer:_____

4.

answer:_____

5. Draw an "X" through any of the following meter signatures that are **not** for compound time:

$$\frac{3}{4} \quad \frac{6}{8} \quad \frac{9}{4} \quad \frac{2}{8} \quad \frac{12}{8} \quad \frac{3}{2} \quad \frac{9}{8} \quad \frac{6}{2} \quad \frac{2}{2} \quad \frac{12}{4}$$

6. Define the following terms:

Simple time:

Measure:

Upbeat:

Meter:

Name_____

Determine the proper meter signature for each of the following rhythms. Place your answer in the blank at the right.

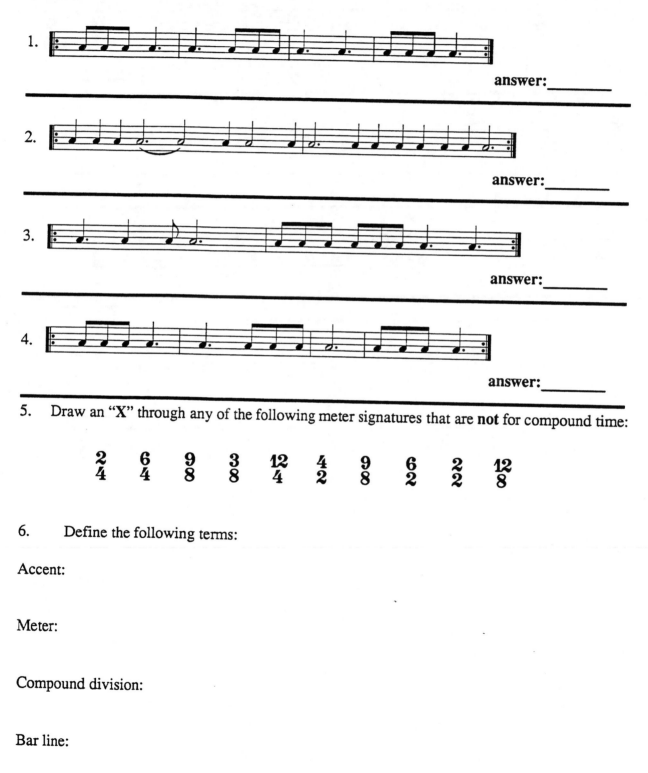

1.

answer:_____

2.

answer:_____

3.

answer:_____

4.

answer:_____

5. Draw an "X" through any of the following meter signatures that are **not** for compound time:

$$\frac{2}{4} \qquad \frac{6}{4} \qquad \frac{9}{8} \qquad \frac{3}{8} \qquad \frac{12}{4} \qquad \frac{4}{2} \qquad \frac{9}{8} \qquad \frac{6}{2} \qquad \frac{2}{2} \qquad \frac{12}{8}$$

6. Define the following terms:

Accent:

Meter:

Compound division:

Bar line:

Name_____

Determine the proper meter signature for each of the following rhythms. Place your answer in the blank at the right.

1.

answer:_____

2.

answer:_____

3.

answer:_____

Write one measure of notes corresponding to the beat of the given meter signature and one measure of notes corresponding to the division of the beat. (See example.)

Ex.

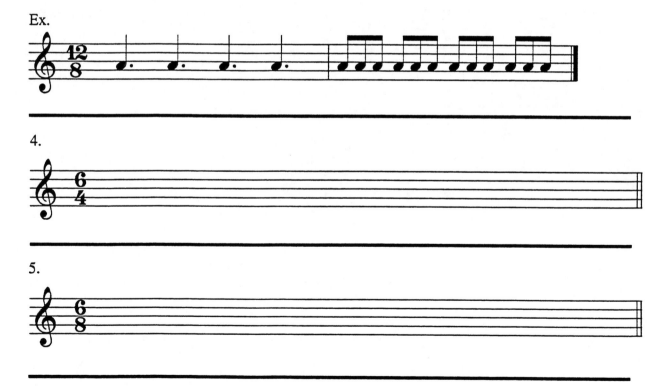

4.

5.

Rewrite the following measures with properly placed beams.

6.

7.

8.

9.

Name_____

Determine the proper meter signature for each of the following rhythms. Place your answer in the blank at the right.

1.   answer:_____

2.   answer:_____

3.   answer:_____

Write one measure of notes corresponding to the beat of the given meter signature and one measure of notes corresponding to the division of the beat. (See example.)

Ex.

4.

5.

Rewrite the following measures with properly placed beams.

6.

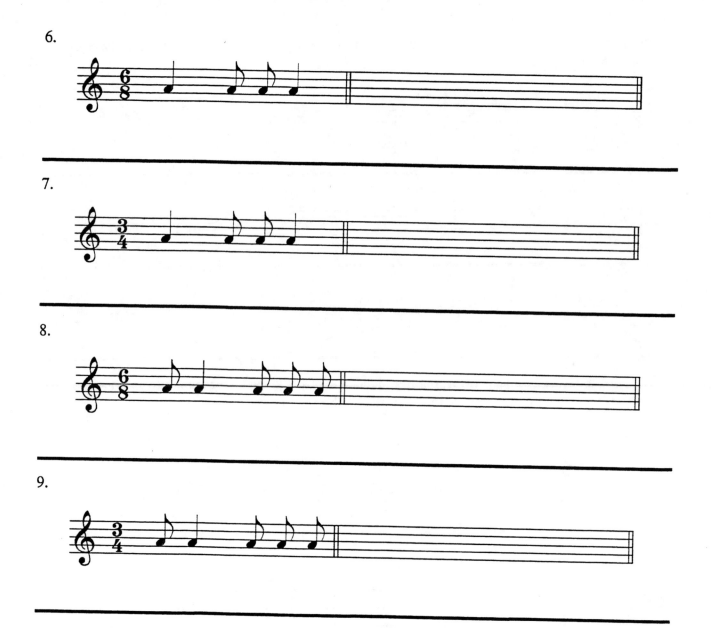

7.

8.

9.

Name_____

Each of the following notes are either a half step or a whole step apart. Check the correct answer.

1. Half_____Whole_____

2. Half_____Whole_____

3. Half_____Whole_____

4. Half_____Whole_____

5. Write the note that is the **enharmonic equivalent** of each of the following notes:

6. Define the following terms:

Key signature:

Double sharp:

Natural:

QUIZ-Chapter 5b-Accidentals

Name_____

Each of the following notes are either a half step or a whole step apart. Check the correct answer.

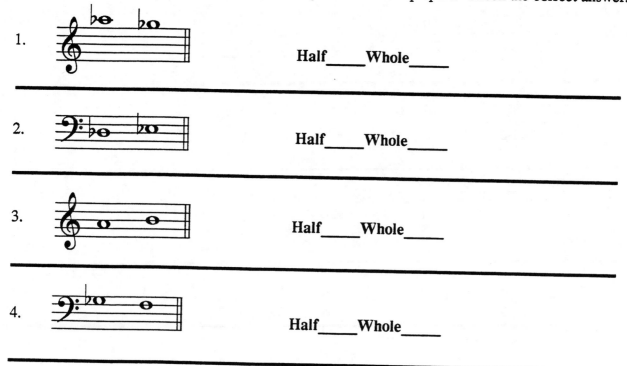

1.   Half_____Whole_____

2.   Half_____Whole_____

3.   Half_____Whole_____

4.   Half_____Whole_____

5.   Write the note that is the **enharmonic equivalent** of each of the following notes:

6.   Define the following terms:

Double flat:

Sharp:

Key signature:

Name_____

Each of the following is either a half step or a whole step. Check the correct answer.

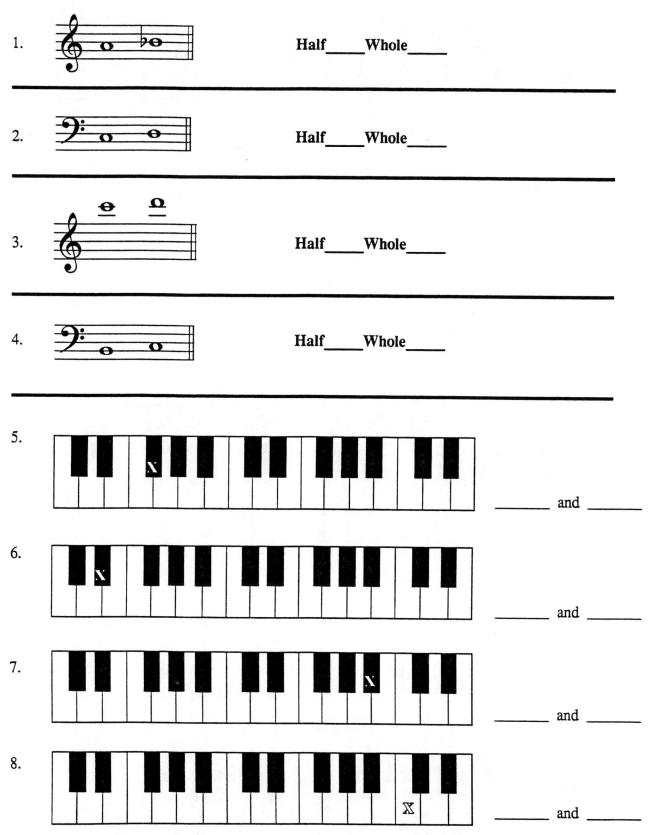

1.　　　　　　　　　　　　　Half_____Whole_____

2.　　　　　　　　　　　　　Half_____Whole_____

3.　　　　　　　　　　　　　Half_____Whole_____

4.　　　　　　　　　　　　　Half_____Whole_____

5.　　　　　　　　　　　　　_____ and _____

6.　　　　　　　　　　　　　_____ and _____

7.　　　　　　　　　　　　　_____ and _____

8.　　　　　　　　　　　　　_____ and _____

QUIZ-Chapter 5d-Accidentals

Name____________

Each of the following is either a half step or a whole step. Check the correct answer.

1.

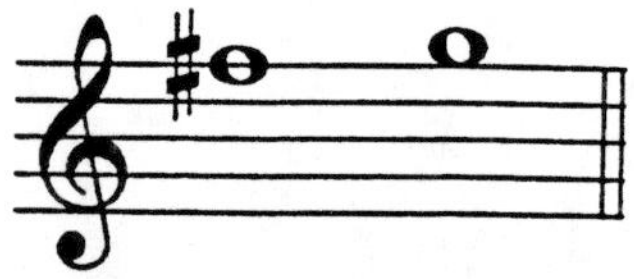

Half____**Whole**____

2.

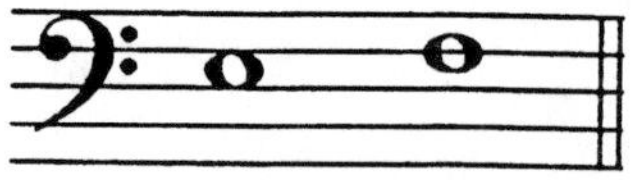

Half____**Whole**____

3.

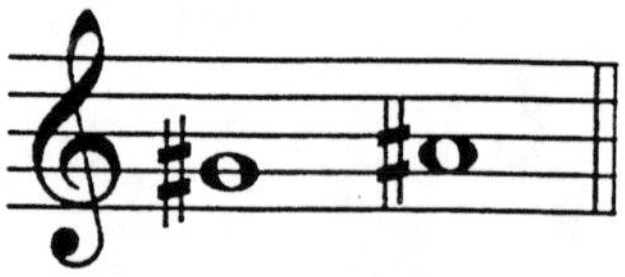

Half____**Whole**____

4.

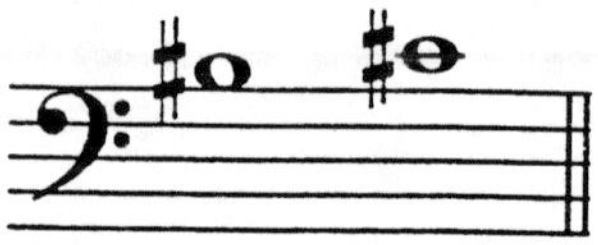

Half____**Whole**____

5.

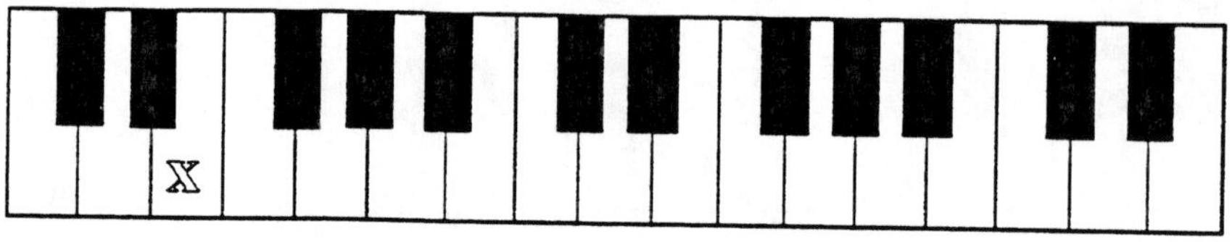

______ and ______

6.

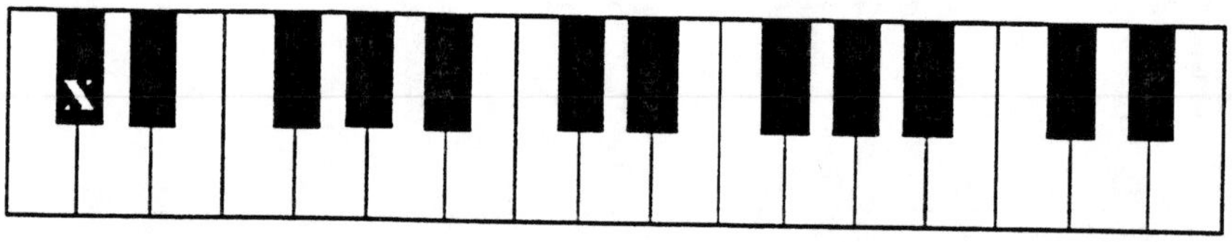

______ and ______

7.

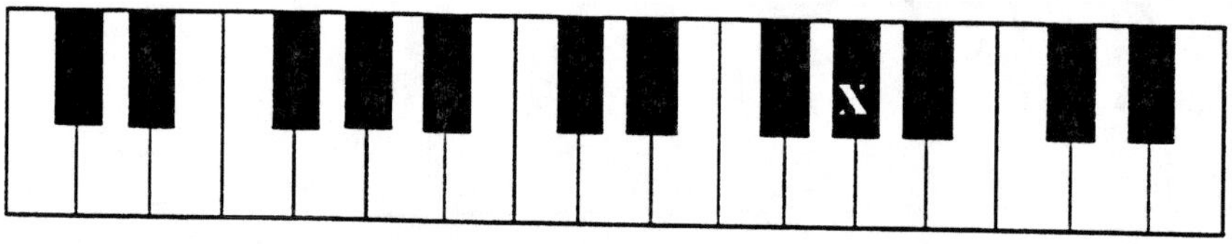

______ and ______

8.

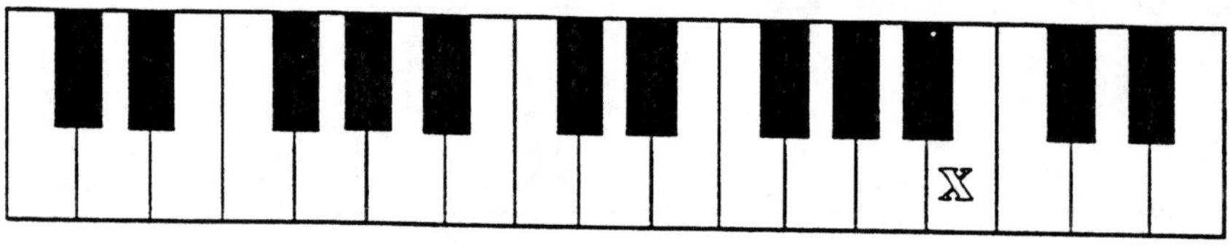

______ and ______

Name_____

Each of the following major scales has one incorrect note. Find the wrong note and place its number in the blank at the right.

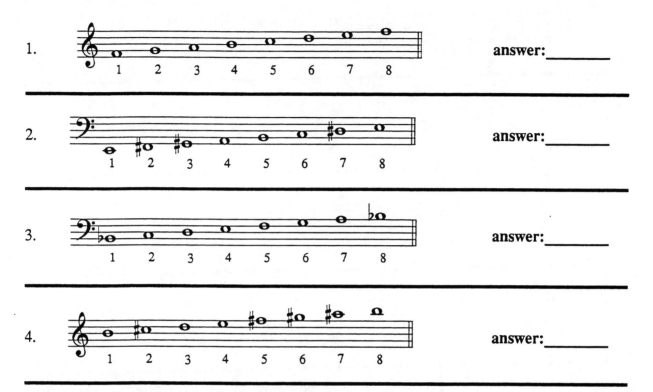

1.   answer:_____

2.   answer:_____

3.   answer:_____

4.   answer:_____

5. Write a major scale using the given note as tonic and adding accidentals as needed. Show the key signature for the scale on the staff beneath it.

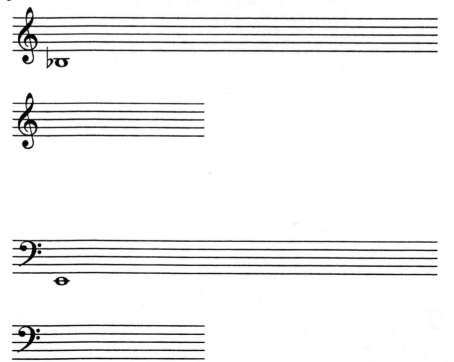

Name_____

Each of the following major scales has one incorrect note. Find the wrong note and place its number in the blank at the right.

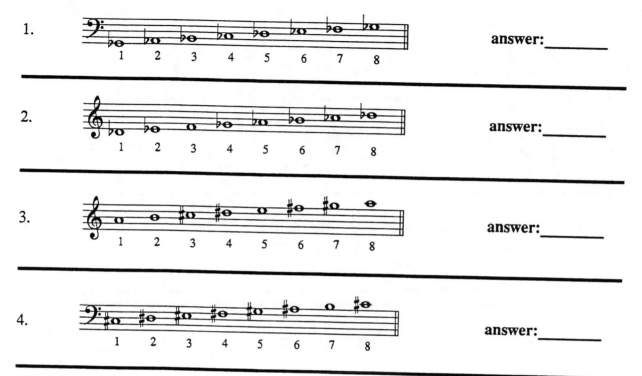

1.   **answer:**_____

2.   **answer:**_____

3.   **answer:**_____

4.   **answer:**_____

5. Write a major scale using the given note as tonic and adding accidentals as needed. Show the key signature for the scale on the staff beneath it.

Name_____

Write the following major scales placing accidentals on notes as needed. Show the key signature for the scale in the space to the right.

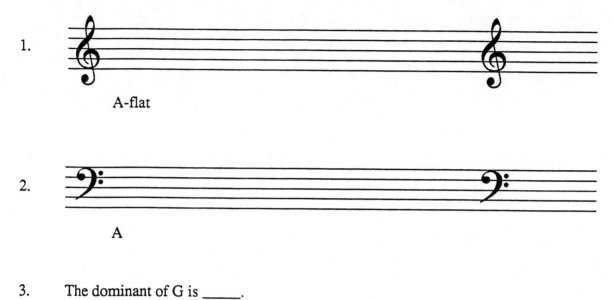

1.

   A-flat

2.

   A

3.   The dominant of G is _____.

4.   The dominant of E♭ is _____.

The following melodies are in the key of C major. Indicate the scale degree of each note using either solfeggio syllables (Do, Re, Mi, etc.) or numbers.

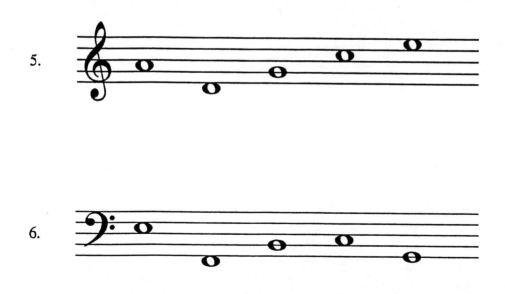

5.

6.

QUIZ-Chapter 6d-Major Keys

Name_____

Write the following major scales placing accidentals on notes as needed. Show the key signature for the scale in the space to the right.

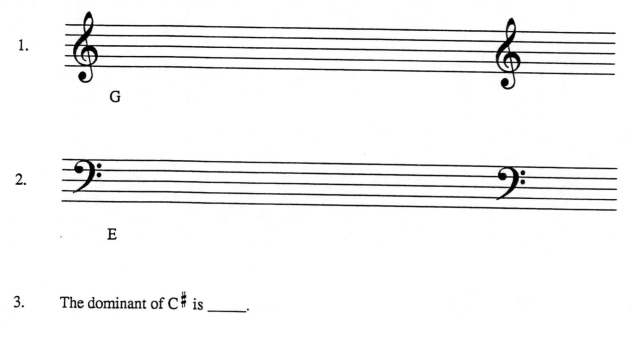

1. G

2. E

3. The dominant of C# is _____.

4. The dominant of A is _____.

The following melodies are in the key of F major. Indicate the scale degree of each note using either solfeggio syllables (Do, Re, Mi, etc.) or numbers.

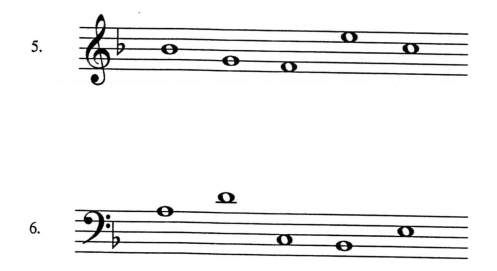

5.

6.

Name_____

In each group of five intervals all but one are the same size. Determine the different interval and place your answer in the blank at the right.

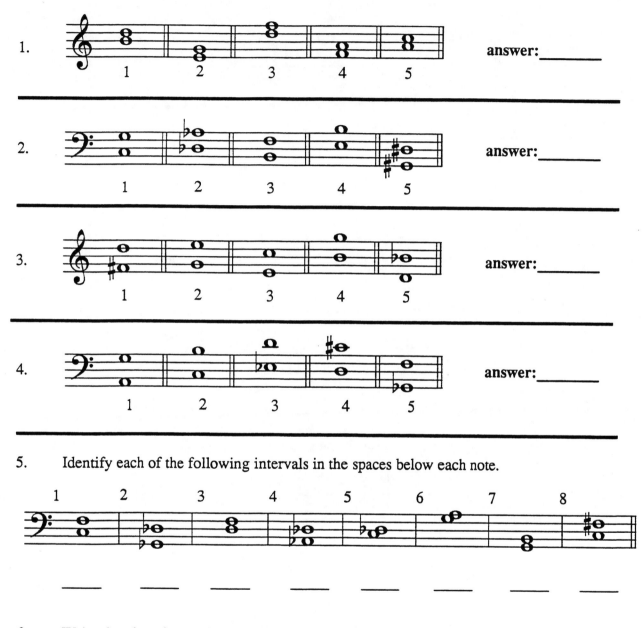

1.

answer:_____

2.

answer:_____

3.

answer:_____

4.

answer:_____

5.   Identify each of the following intervals in the spaces below each note.

6.   Write the given interval <u>above and below</u> each of the following notes:

P4   **M3**   **M6**   **P5**

QUIZ-Chapter 7b-Intervals

Name_____

In each group of five intervals all but one are the same size. Determine the different interval and place your answer in the blank at the right.

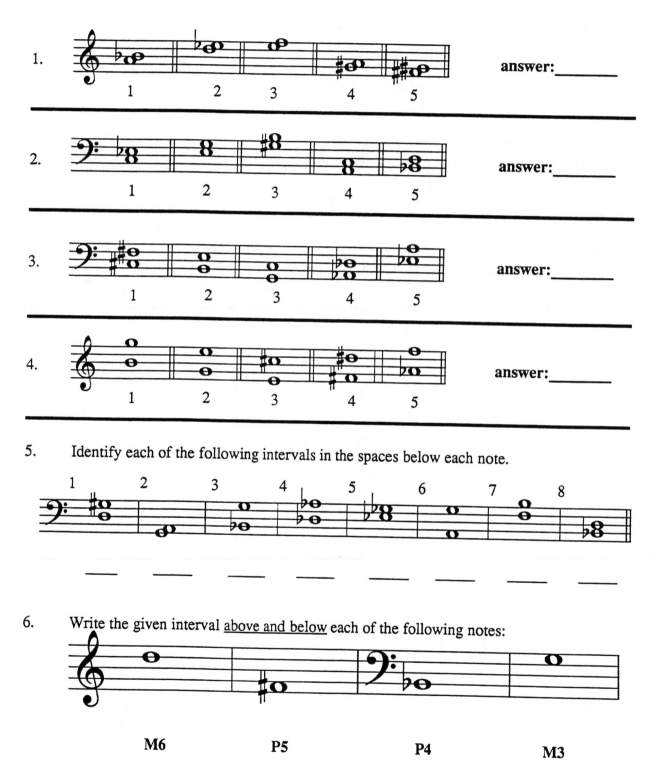

1.   answer:_____

2.   answer:_____

3.   answer:_____

4.   answer:_____

5.   Identify each of the following intervals in the spaces below each note.

6.   Write the given interval <u>above and below</u> each of the following notes:

M6   P5   P4   M3

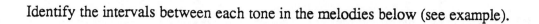

QUIZ-Chapter 7c-Intervals

Name_____

Identify the intervals between each tone in the melodies below (see example).

1.

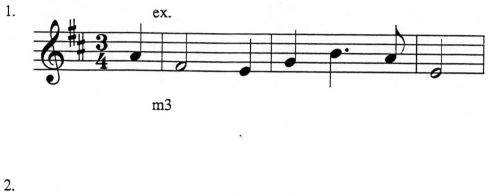

2.

3.   Write the given interval <u>above and below</u> each of the following notes:

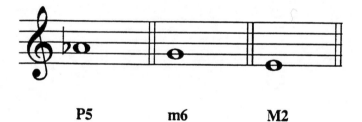

P5   **m6**   **M2**

4.   Define: Inversion of an interval

35

QUIZ-Chapter 7d-Intervals

Name_____

Identify the intervals between each tone in the melodies below (see example).

1.   ex.

P5

2.

3.   Write the given interval <u>above and below</u> each of the following notes:

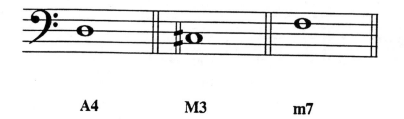

   A4   M3   m7

4.   Define: Enharmonic interval

Name_____

Each of the following minor scales has one incorrect note. Find the wrong note and place its number in the blank at the right.

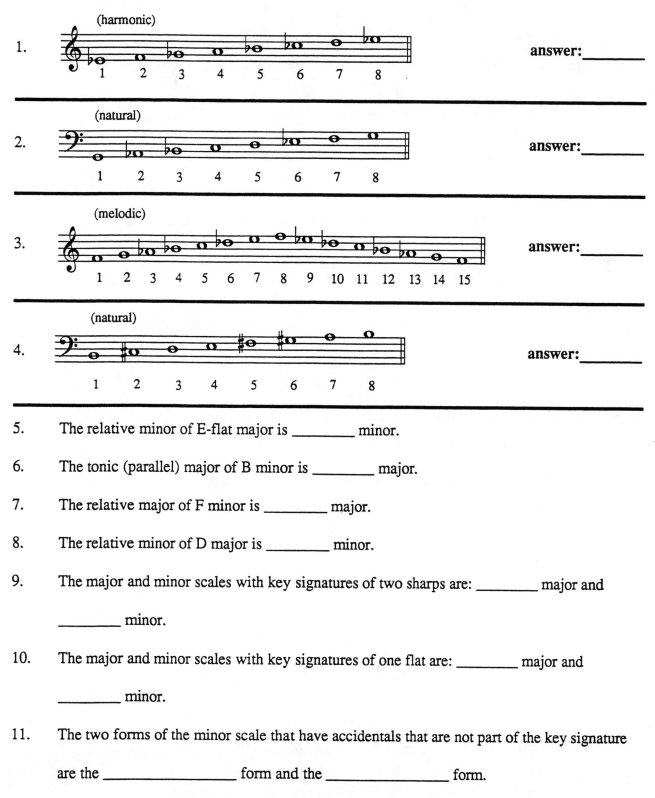

1.

answer:_____

2.

answer:_____

3.

answer:_____

4.

answer:_____

5.   The relative minor of E-flat major is _____ minor.

6.   The tonic (parallel) major of B minor is _____ major.

7.   The relative major of F minor is _____ major.

8.   The relative minor of D major is _____ minor.

9.   The major and minor scales with key signatures of two sharps are: _____ major and

_____ minor.

10.   The major and minor scales with key signatures of one flat are: _____ major and

_____ minor.

11.   The two forms of the minor scale that have accidentals that are not part of the key signature

are the _____ form and the _____ form.

QUIZ-Chapter 8b-Minor Keys

Name_____

Each of the following minor scales has one incorrect note. Find the wrong note and place its number in the blank at the right.

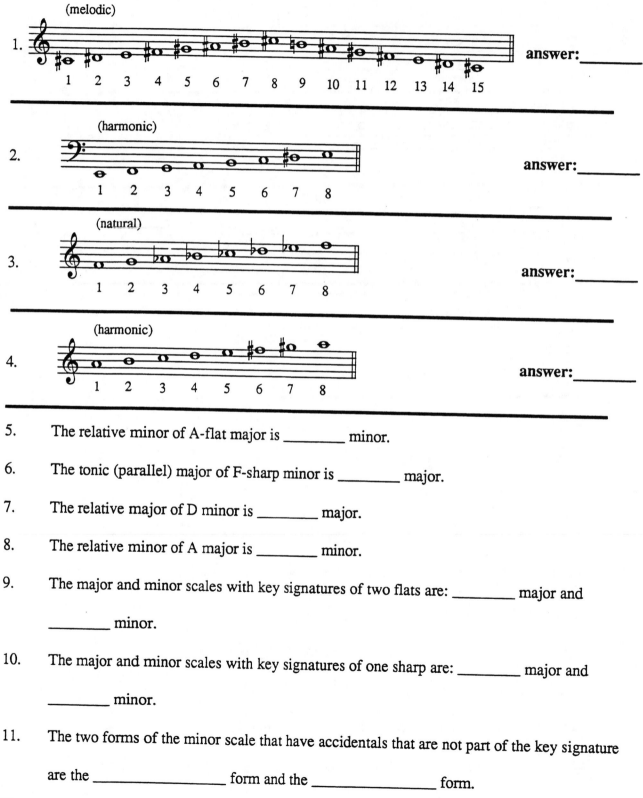

1. (melodic)

   1 2 3 4 5 6 7 8 9 10 11 12 13 14 15   answer:_____

2. (harmonic)

   1 2 3 4 5 6 7 8   answer:_____

3. (natural)

   1 2 3 4 5 6 7 8   answer:_____

4. (harmonic)

   1 2 3 4 5 6 7 8   answer:_____

5. The relative minor of A-flat major is _____ minor.

6. The tonic (parallel) major of F-sharp minor is _____ major.

7. The relative major of D minor is _____ major.

8. The relative minor of A major is _____ minor.

9. The major and minor scales with key signatures of two flats are: _____ major and

   _____ minor.

10. The major and minor scales with key signatures of one sharp are: _____ major and

   _____ minor.

11. The two forms of the minor scale that have accidentals that are not part of the key signature

   are the _____ form and the _____ form.

Name_____

Write the following minor scales placing accidentals on notes as needed. Show the key signature for the scale in the space at the right.

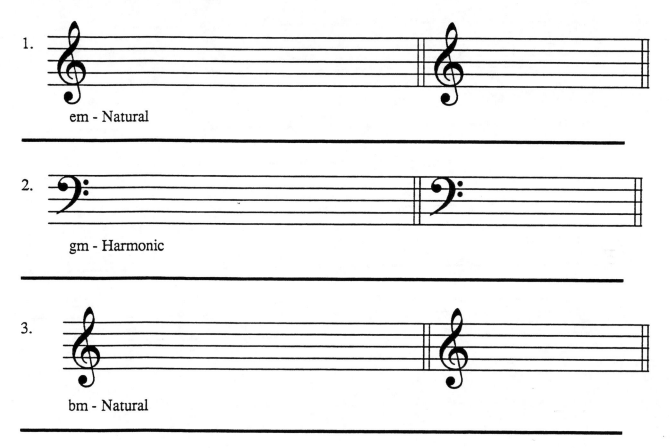

1.

em - Natural

2.

gm - Harmonic

3.

bm - Natural

4.   The interval between the tonic of a minor key and the tonic of its relative major is _____.

5.   The difference in number of sharps (or flats) between a minor key and its parallel major is

_____.

6.   Define: Circle of fifths

QUIZ-Chapter 8d-Minor Keys

Name_____

Write the following minor scales placing accidentals on notes as needed. Show the key signature for the scale in the space at the right.

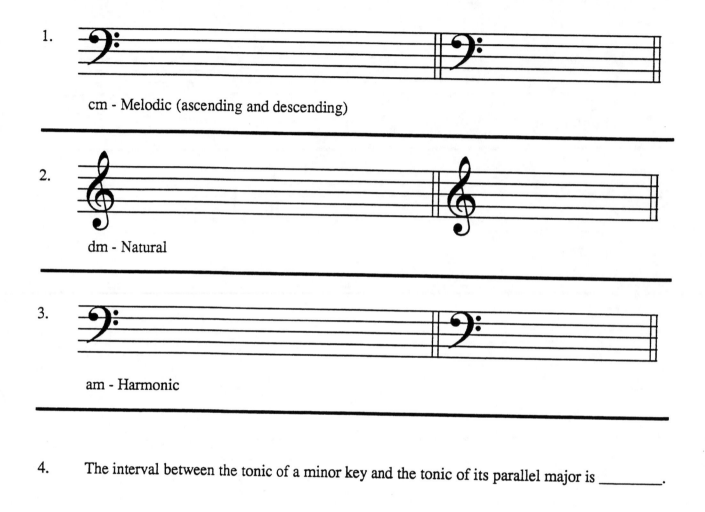

1.

cm - Melodic (ascending and descending)

2.

dm - Natural

3.

am - Harmonic

4.   The interval between the tonic of a minor key and the tonic of its parallel major is _____.

5.   The difference in number of sharps (or flats) between a minor key and its relative major is

_____.

6.   Define: Circle of fifths

Name_____

1.   Add one note to each of the following to make a major triad:

2.   Add one note to each of the following to make a minor triad:

3.   Write the popular music chord symbol above each of the following chords:

4.   Write the chords requested below each popular chord symbol:

G^7 D F_{MI} C_{MI}^7 F+

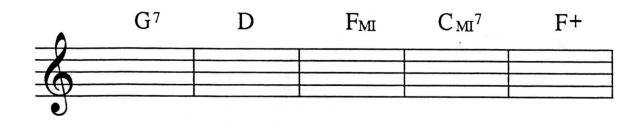

QUIZ-Chapter 9b-Chords

Name_____

1.   Add one note to each of the following to make a major triad:

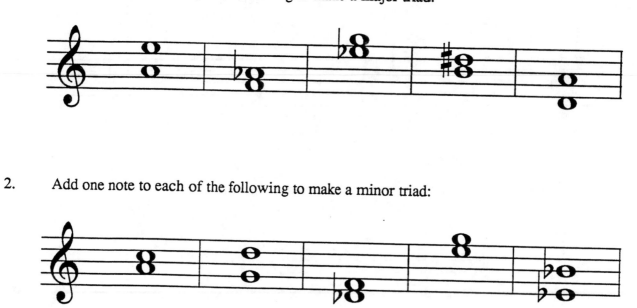

2.   Add one note to each of the following to make a minor triad:

3.   Write the popular music chord symbol above each of the following chords:

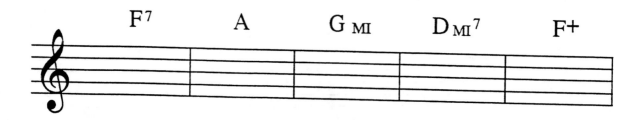

4.   Write the chords requested below each popular chord symbol:

F⁷   A   G MI   D MI⁷   F+

Name_____

Identify the expanded chords and write them in simplest position (see example).

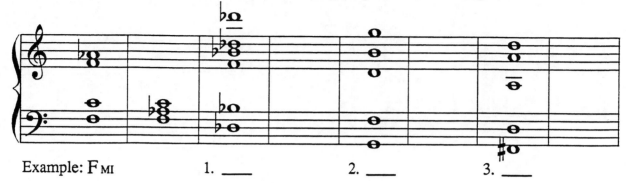

Example: F MI   1. ____   2. ____   3. ____

4.   Form major triads on the following roots:

5.   Form minor seventh chords on the following roots:

Write the following triads in all inversions (see example).

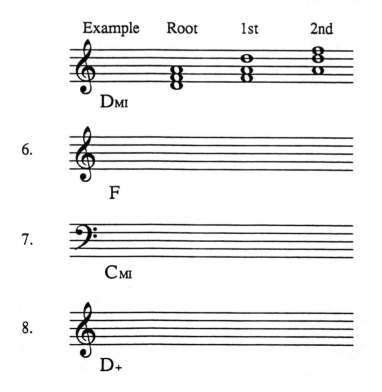

Example   Root   1st   2nd

D MI

6.   F

7.   C MI

8.   D+

QUIZ-Chapter 9d-Chords

Name_____

Identify the expanded chords and write them in simplest position (see example).

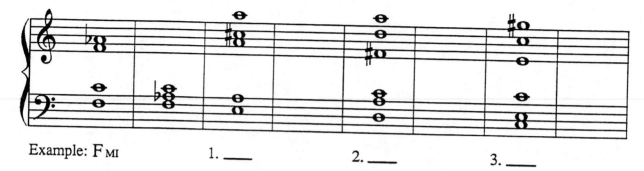

Example: F MI   1. ___   2. ___   3. ___

4.   Form major-minor seventh chords on the following roots (see example):

5.   Form minor triads on the following roots:

Write the following triads in all inversions (see example).

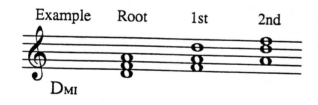

6.

7.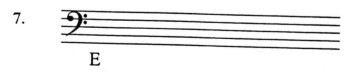

8.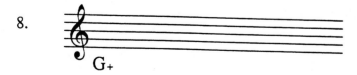

QUIZ-Chapter 10a-Harmony

Name_____

1. Write the three primary triads in each of the following keys. Remember to use the proper key signature.

F minor (harmonic form)

E-flat major

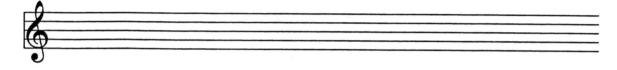

2. Write the indicated chords on the staff below the melody. Do a roman numeral analysis of the chords in this song. Indicate all "circle progressions" by drawing a line between the chords.

QUIZ-Chapter 10b-Harmony

Name_____

1. Write the three primary triads in each of the following keys. Remember to use the proper key signature.

D minor (harmonic form)

A-flat major

2. Write the indicated chords on the staff below the melody. Do a roman numeral analysis of the chords in this song. Indicate all "circle progressions" by drawing a line between the chords.

G:

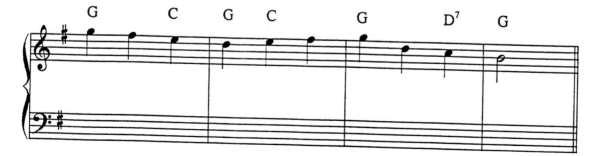

QUIZ-Chapter 10c-Harmony

Name_____

1. Write the three primary triads in each of the following keys. Remember to use the proper key signature.

B minor (harmonic form)

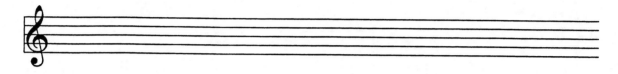

A major

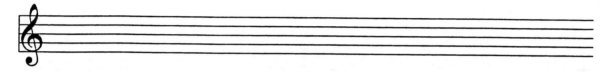

2. Write the indicated chords on the staff below the melody. Do a roman numeral analysis of the chords in this song. Indicate all "circle progressions" by drawing a line between the chords.

QUIZ-Chapter 10d-Harmony

Name_____

1. Write the three primary triads in each of the following keys. Remember to use the proper key signature.

E major

C minor (harmonic form)

2. Write the indicated chords on the staff below the melody. Do a roman numeral analysis of the chords in this song. Indicate all "circle progressions" by drawing a line between the chords.

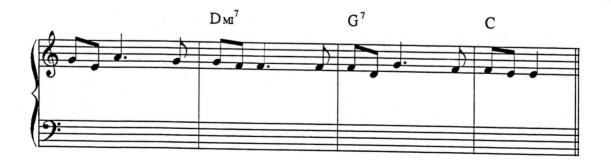

QUIZ-Chapter 11a-Harmonizing and Composing
Songs and Accompaniments

Name_____

1. Fill in the chords with the proper rhythm in the song "Barbara Allen" on the following page.

    Do a roman numeral analysis. (See the first chord for an example.)

2. Circle all nonharmonic notes in the melody of "Barbara Allen."

3. The harmonic cadence in measure four (A) is a(n) _____ cadence.

4. The harmonic cadence in the final measure (D) is a(n) _____ cadence.

5. The harmonic rhythm throughout the song is _____ (note value) except

    measure _____ which is _____ (note value).

"Barbara Allen"

50

QUIZ-Chapter 11b-Harmonizing and Composing
Songs and Accompaniments

Name_____

1.   Fill in the chords with the proper rhythm in the song "Barbara Allen" on the following page.

     Do a roman numeral analysis. (See the first chord for an example.)

2.   Circle all nonharmonic notes in the melody of "Barbara Allen."

3.   The harmonic cadence in measure four (F) is a(n) _____ cadence.

4.   The harmonic cadence in the final measure (B-flat) is a(n) _____ cadence.

5.   The harmonic rhythm throughout the song is _____ (note value) except

     measure _____ which is _____ (note value).

"Barbara Allen"

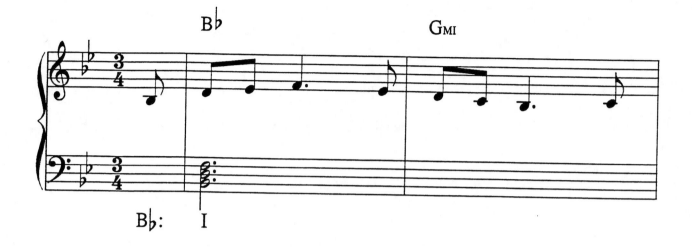

Name_____

1.   Fill in the chords with the proper rhythm in the song "Simple Gifts" on the following page.

    Do a roman numeral analysis. (See the first chord for an example.)

2.   Circle all nonharmonic notes in the melody of "Simple Gifts."

3.   Mark the end of the first phrase. What is the harmonic cadence here?

4.   Mark the end of the second phrase. What is the harmonic cadence here?

5.   Graph the contour of the first phrase above the melody.

"Simple Gifts"

F: I

Name_____

1.   Fill in the chords with the proper rhythm in the song "Simple Gifts" on the following page.

     Do a roman numeral analysis. (See the first chord for an example.)

2.   Circle all nonharmonic notes in the melody of "Simple Gifts."

3.   Mark the end of the first phrase. What is the harmonic cadence here?

4.   Mark the end of the second phrase. What is the harmonic cadence here?

5.   Graph the contour of the second phrase above the melody.

"Simple Gifts"

A: I

Keys for Chapter Quizzes

Name_____

Add up the number of quarter note beats in each pattern and select the correct answer from the five choices given. Place your answer in the blank at the right.

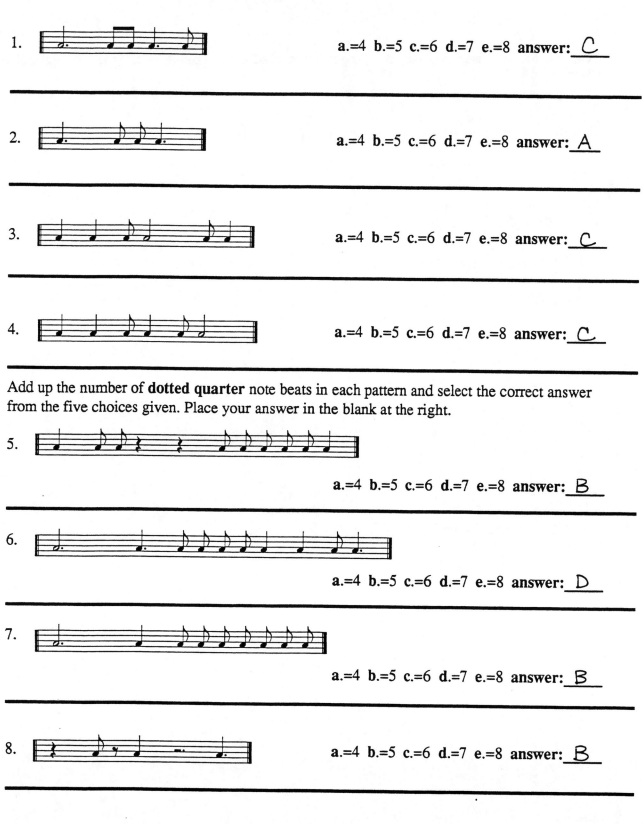

1.   **a.**=4 **b.**=5 **c.**=6 **d.**=7 **e.**=8 **answer:** _C_

2.   **a.**=4 **b.**=5 **c.**=6 **d.**=7 **e.**=8 **answer:** _A_

3.   **a.**=4 **b.**=5 **c.**=6 **d.**=7 **e.**=8 **answer:** _C_

4.   **a.**=4 **b.**=5 **c.**=6 **d.**=7 **e.**=8 **answer:** _C_

Add up the number of **dotted quarter** note beats in each pattern and select the correct answer from the five choices given. Place your answer in the blank at the right.

5.   **a.**=4 **b.**=5 **c.**=6 **d.**=7 **e.**=8 **answer:** _B_

6.   **a.**=4 **b.**=5 **c.**=6 **d.**=7 **e.**=8 **answer:** _D_

7.   **a.**=4 **b.**=5 **c.**=6 **d.**=7 **e.**=8 **answer:** _B_

8.   **a.**=4 **b.**=5 **c.**=6 **d.**=7 **e.**=8 **answer:** _B_

9. Define the following terms:

Stem:

A vertical line drawn upward or downward from a notehead

Flag:

The curved, shaded line extending from the end of a stem used to indicate an eighth or shorter note.

Beam:

A broad, straight line connecting two or more eighth notes.

Dot:

A small symbol that is placed beside the head of a note that increases the duration by one-half.

10. Write examples of the following musical symbols:

Dotted half note:

Eighth rest:

Two quarter notes with tie:

Pair of eighth notes with beam:

QUIZ-Chapter 1b-Rhythm

Name_____

Add up the number of quarter note beats in each pattern and select the correct answer from the five choices given. Place your answer in the blank at the right.

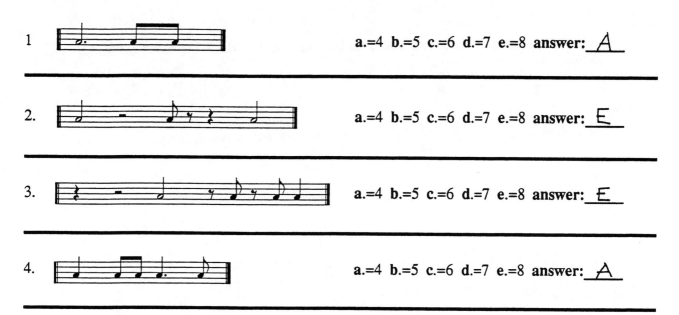

1   a.=4 b.=5 c.=6 d.=7 e.=8 answer: _A_

2.   a.=4 b.=5 c.=6 d.=7 e.=8 answer: _E_

3.   a.=4 b.=5 c.=6 d.=7 e.=8 answer: _E_

4.   a.=4 b.=5 c.=6 d.=7 e.=8 answer: _A_

Add up the number of **dotted quarter** note beats in each pattern and select the correct answer from the five choices given. Place your answer in the blank at the right.

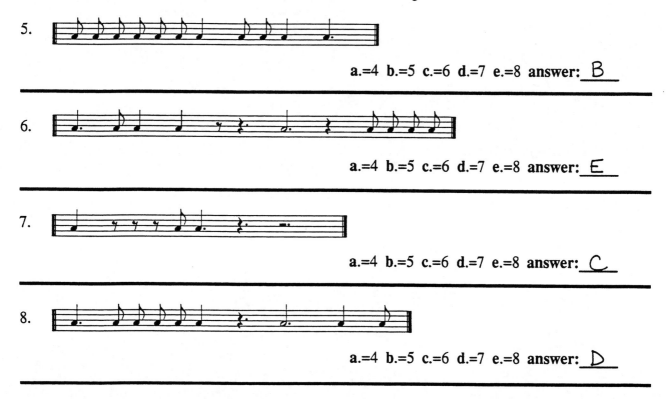

5.   a.=4 b.=5 c.=6 d.=7 e.=8 answer: _B_

6.   a.=4 b.=5 c.=6 d.=7 e.=8 answer: _E_

7.   a.=4 b.=5 c.=6 d.=7 e.=8 answer: _C_

8.   a.=4 b.=5 c.=6 d.=7 e.=8 answer: _D_

9. Define the following terms:

Rest:

A symbol used to indicate silence in music.

Tie:

A curved line conecting two notes that indicates that they are to be played as a single note.

Beat:

The steady pulse of music. Beats form the basis of musical time.

Flag:

The curved, shaded line extending from the end of a stem used to indicate an eighth or shorter note.

10. Write examples of the following musical symbols:

Single eighth note:

Dotted half note:

Quarter rest:

Two half notes with tie:

Name_____

For each note given below, draw the equivalent rest (see example).

For each rest given below, draw the equivalent note.

6. Define the following terms:

Notehead:

The round part of a note that is used to indicate the pitch of the note.

Beam:

A broad, straight line connecting two or more eighth notes.

Repeat signs:

Any one of the symbols used to indicate the restatement of a musical idea or section.

Tempo:

The speed of the beat in music, which may be expressed in general terms or in beats per minute.

Simple division:

The division of the beat into two equal parts.

QUIZ-Chapter 1d-Rhythm

Name_____

For each note given below draw the equivalent rest (see example).

Ex.

1.

2.

For each rest given below draw the equivalent note.

3.

4.

5.

6. Define the following terms:

Beat:

Flag:

Dot: **A small symbol that is placed beside the head of a note that increases the duration by one half.**

Compound division:

Rhythmic pattern:

1. Draw the clef indicated and write the note:

D quarter note	E eighth note	C half note	G dotted eighth	2 B's eighth notes
Bass clef	Treble clef	Bass clef	Treble clef	with beam
				Bass clef

2. Name the given notes (A, B, C, D, E, F, G) on the blanks below:

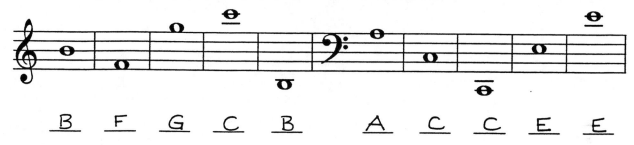

B   F   G   C   B   A   C   C   E   E

3. Define the following terms:

Middle C:

The C nearest to the middle of the piano keyboard.

Ledger line:

A small line written above or below the staff to extend its range.

Grand staff:

A combination of the treble and bass clefs that is commonly used to notate keyboard music.

Slur:

A curved line connecting two or more notes, indicating that they are to be played smoothly.

4. Write a note an octave above or below the given notes as indicated:

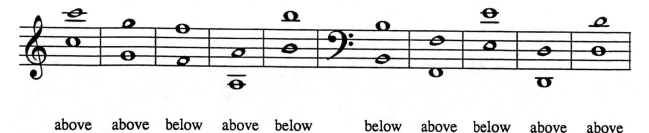

above   above   below   above   below   below   above   below   above   above

QUIZ-Chapter 2b-Pitch

Name_____

1. Draw the clef indicated and write the note:

F quarter note
Bass clef

G eighth note
Treble clef

B half note
Bass clef

C dotted eighth
Treble clef

2 G's eighth notes
with beam
Bass clef

2. Name the given notes (A, B, C, D, E, F, G) on the blanks below:

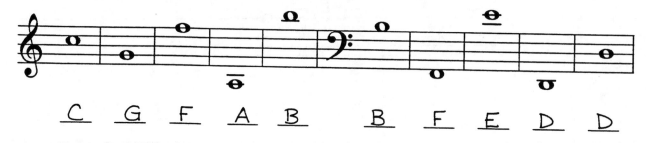

C G F A B   B F E D D

3. Define the following terms:

Clef:

A symbol placed at the beginning of the staff to indicate the names of the lines and spaces.

Octave:

The interval between two adjacent notes of the same name.

Staff:

A group of five horizontal lines on which music is notated.

Grand Staff:

A combination of the treble and bass clefs that is commonly used to notate keyboard music.

4. Write a note an octave above or below the given notes as indicated:

above above below below above   below below above above below

Name_____

1. Draw the clef indicated and write the note:

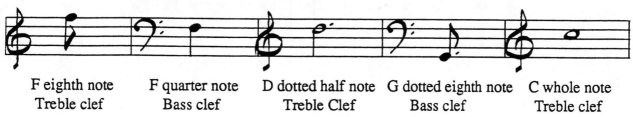

   F eighth note   F quarter note   D dotted half note G dotted eighth note C whole note
   Treble clef   Bass clef   Treble Clef   Bass clef   Treble clef

2. Name the given notes (A, B, C, D, E, F, G) on the blank below:

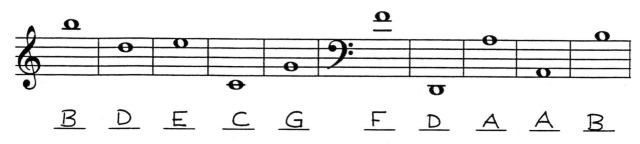

   B   D   E   C   G   F   D   A   A   B

3. Define the following terms:

Pitch:

  The "highness" or "lowness" of a musical tone.

Treble clef:

  The most common clef in music. It is a stylized letter "G" that indicates that the second line of the staff is to be G.

Octave:

  The interval between two adjacent notes of the same name. The name comes from the Latin word for eight, denoting the eight pitch classes contained within the interval.

Staff:

  A group of five horizontal lines on which music is notated.

4. Mark the following notes on the keyboard:

1. B

2. C

3. G

4. F

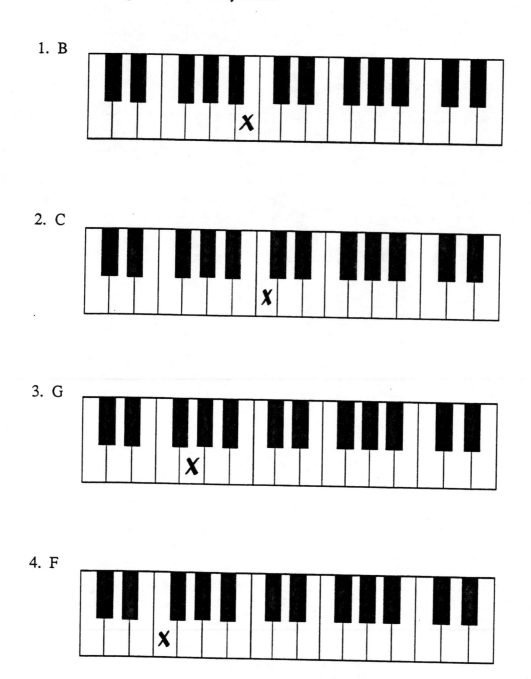

Name_____

1. Draw the clef indicated and write the note:

E two eighth   A dotted half note   D dotted quarter   C whole note   F two eighth
notes with beam   Bass clef   quarter note   Bass clef   notes with beam
Treble clef   Treble Clef   Treble clef

2. Name the given notes (A, B, C, D, E, F, G) on the blank below:

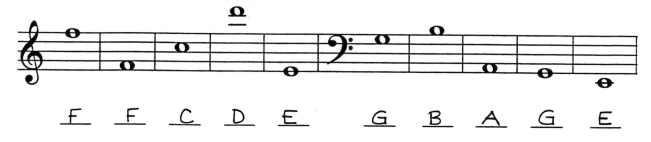

F   F   C   D   E   G   B   A   G   E

3. Define the following terms:

Slur:

A curved line connecting two or more notes, indicating that they are to be played smoothly. Also used to connect notes that are sung on one syllable.

Bass clef:

A common clef in music. The bass clef is a stylized letter "F" that indicates that the fourth line of the staff is named "F".

Middle C:

The C nearest the middle of the piano keyboard. This note is an important point of reference because it is on the ledger line between the treble and bass staves on the grand staff.

Ledger line:

A small line written above or below the staff to extend its range.

4.   Mark the following notes on the keyboard:

1. A

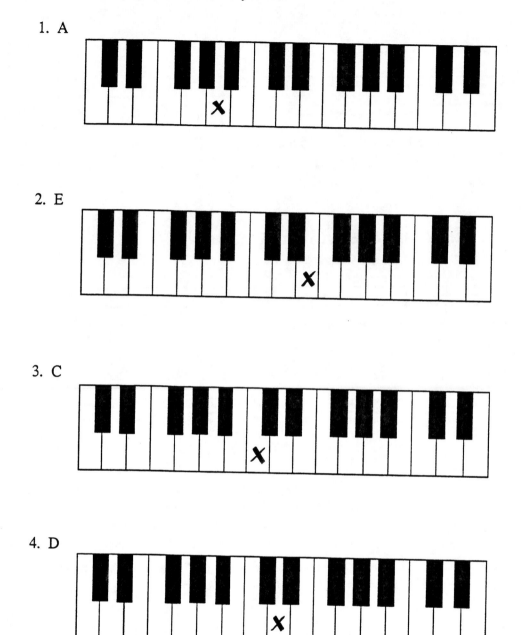

2. E

3. C

4. D

Name_____

Determine the proper meter signature for each of the following rhythms. Place your answer in the blank at the right. (There may be more than one correct answer.)

1. answer: $\frac{3}{8}$

2. answer: $\frac{3}{4}$

3. answer: $\frac{4}{2}$

4. answer: $\frac{2}{8}$

5. Give the note value for the beat and the division of the beat for each of the following meter signatures (**Draw the note and give its name**):

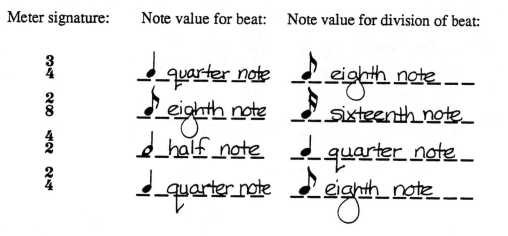

Meter signature:	Note value for beat:	Note value for division of beat:
$\frac{3}{4}$	quarter note	eighth note
$\frac{2}{8}$	eighth note	sixteenth note
$\frac{4}{2}$	half note	quarter note
$\frac{2}{4}$	quarter note	eighth note

6. Define: Accent

Emphasis on one note.

QUIZ-Chapter 3b-Simple Meter

Name_____

Determine the proper meter signature for each of the following rhythms. Place your answer in the blank at the right. (There may be more than one correct answer.)

1. answer: 4/4

2. answer: 3/4

3. answer: 3/2

4. answer: 2/4

5. Give the note value for the beat and the division of the beat for each of the following meter signatures (**Draw the note and give its name**):

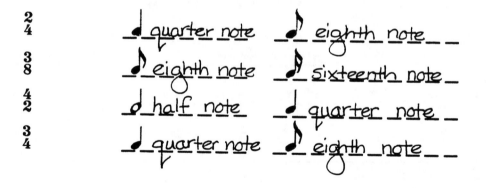

Meter signature:	Note value for beat:	Note value for division of beat:
2/4	♩ quarter note	♪ eighth note
3/8	♪ eighth note	♫ sixteenth note
4/2	♩ half note	♩ quarter note
3/4	♩ quarter note	♪ eighth note

6. Define: Measure

> **One unit of meter, consisting of a number of accented and unaccented beats. A measure is indicated in music notation by bar lines.**

QUIZ-Chapter 3c-Simple Meter

Name_____

Determine the proper meter signature for each of the following rhythms. Place your answer in the blank at the right. (There may be more than one correct answer.)

1. answer: 4/4 or 2/2

2. answer: 3/2

3. answer: 4/8 or 2/4

4. answer: 3/4

Create two measures of music for the following meter signatures. The first measure should contain note values corresponding to the beat and the second measure should contain note values corresponding to the divisions of the beat. (See the example which follows.)

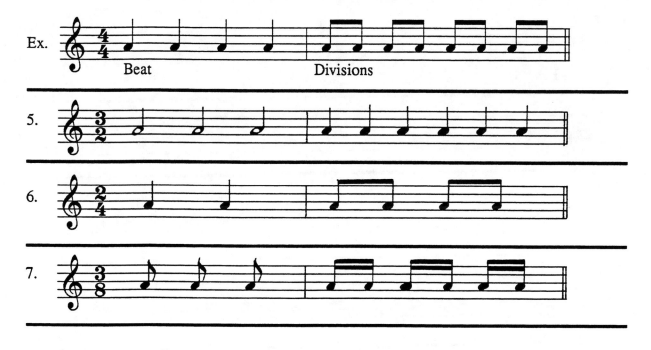

Ex.   Beat   Divisions

5.

6.

7.

8. Define: Upbeat

> **The note or notes that occur at the beginning of a phrase before the beginning of the first full measure.**

73

Name_____

Determine the proper meter signature for each of the following rhythms. Place your answer in the blank at the right. (There may be more than one correct answer.)

1.   answer: $\frac{4}{2}$

2.   answer: $\frac{4}{8}$ or $\frac{2}{4}$

3.   answer: $\frac{3}{4}$

4.   answer: $\frac{3}{8}$

Create two measures of music for the following meter signatures. The first measure should contain note values corresponding to the beat and the second measure should contain note values corresponding to the divisions of the beat. (See the example which follows.)

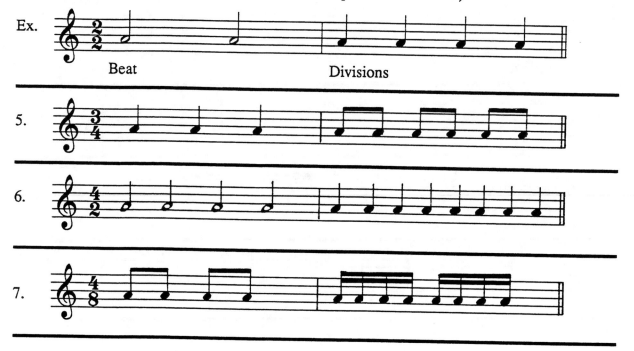

Ex.   Beat   Divisions

5.

6.

7.

8. Define: Cut time

Another name for the 2/2 meter signature. This meter is indicated with a large capital C with a vertical line drawn through it.

Name_____

Determine the proper meter signature for each of the following rhythms. Place your answer in the blank at the right.

1.

answer: $\frac{9}{8}$

2.

answer: $\frac{6}{4}$

3.

answer: $\frac{9}{8}$

4.

answer: $\frac{9}{4}$

5. Draw an "X" through any of the following meter signatures that are **not** for compound time:

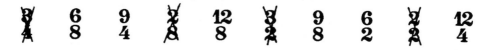

6. Define the following terms:

Simple time:

A meter in which the beat is divided into two equal parts.

Measure:

One unit of meter, consisting of a number of accented and unaccented beats. Indicated by bar lines.

Upbeat:

The note or notes that occur at the beginning of a phrase before the beginning of the first full measure.

Meter:

A regular pattern of accents in the beats of a piece of music.

QUIZ-Chapter 4b-Compound Meter

Name_____

Determine the proper meter signature for each of the following rhythms. Place your answer in the blank at the right.

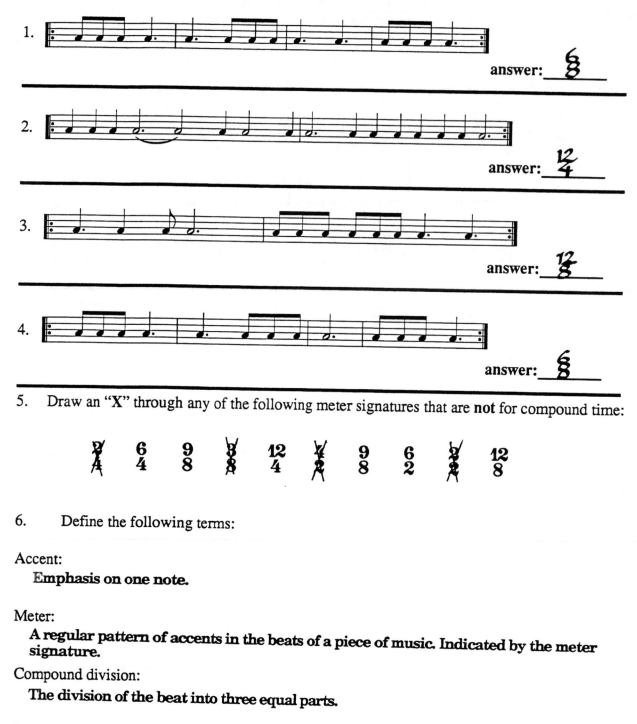

1.

answer:___$\frac{6}{8}$___

2.

answer:___$\frac{12}{4}$___

3.

answer:___$\frac{12}{8}$___

4.

answer:___$\frac{6}{8}$___

5. Draw an "X" through any of the following meter signatures that are **not** for compound time:

$\frac{2}{4}$ $\frac{6}{4}$ $\frac{9}{8}$ $\frac{3}{8}$ $\frac{12}{4}$ $\frac{4}{2}$ $\frac{9}{8}$ $\frac{6}{2}$ $\frac{2}{2}$ $\frac{12}{8}$

6. Define the following terms:

Accent:

Emphasis on one note.

Meter:

A regular pattern of accents in the beats of a piece of music. Indicated by the meter signature.

Compound division:

The division of the beat into three equal parts.

Bar line:

A vertical line drawn across the staff to indicate measures in a musical composition.

QUIZ-Chapter 4c-Compound Meter

Name_____

Determine the proper meter signature for each of the following rhythms. Place your answer in the blank at the right.

1. answer: $\frac{12}{4}$

2. answer: $\frac{6}{8}$

3. answer: $\frac{9}{8}$

Write one measure of notes corresponding to the beat of the given meter signature and one measure of notes corresponding to the division of the beat. (See example.)

Ex.

4.

5.

Rewrite the following measures with properly placed beams.

6.

7.

8.

9.

Name_____

Determine the proper meter signature for each of the following rhythms. Place your answer in the blank at the right.

1.   answer: $\frac{12}{8}$

2.   answer: $\frac{6}{4}$

3.   answer: $\frac{9}{4}$

Write one measure of notes corresponding to the beat of the given meter signature and one measure of notes corresponding to the division of the beat. (See example.)

Ex.

4.

5.

Rewrite the following measures with properly placed beams.

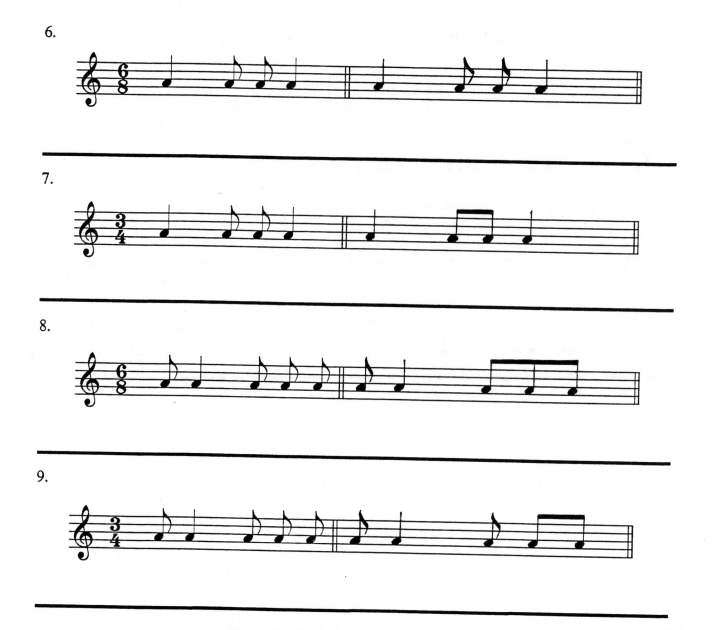

6.

7.

8.

9.

Name_____

Each of the following notes are either a half step or a whole step apart. Check the correct answer.

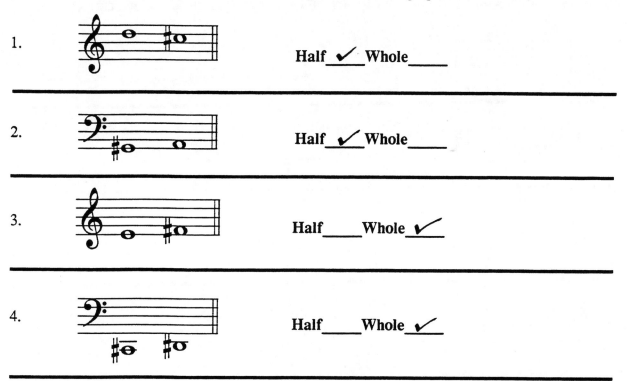

1. Half __✔__ Whole_____

2. Half __✔__ Whole_____

3. Half_____ Whole __✔__

4. Half_____ Whole __✔__

5.   Write the note that is the **enharmonic equivalent** of each of the following notes:

6.   Define the following terms:

Key signature:
   Accidentals at the beginning of a staff that indicate the pitches that will be most common in the piece.

Double sharp:
   A symbol that raises the pitch of a note by a whole step (or two half steps).

Natural:
   A symbol that cancels a previous sharp or flat.

QUIZ-Chapter 5b-Accidentals

Name_____

Each of the following notes are either a half step or a whole step apart. Check the correct answer.

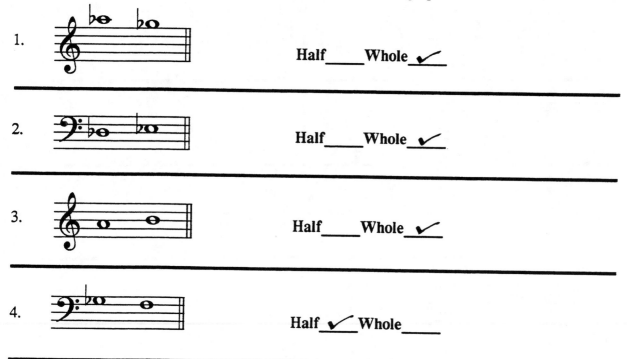

1. Half_____Whole ✓

2. Half_____Whole ✓

3. Half_____Whole ✓

4. Half ✓ Whole_____

5. Write the note that is the **enharmonic equivalent** of each of the following notes:

6. Define the following terms:

Double flat:

A symbol that lowers the pitch of a note by a whole step (or two half steps).

Sharp:

A symbol that raises the pitch of a note by a half step.

Key signature:

Accidentals at the beginning of a staff that indicate the pitches that will be most common in the piece.

QUIZ-Chapter 5c-Accidentals

Name_____

Each of the following is either a half step or a whole step. Check the correct answer.

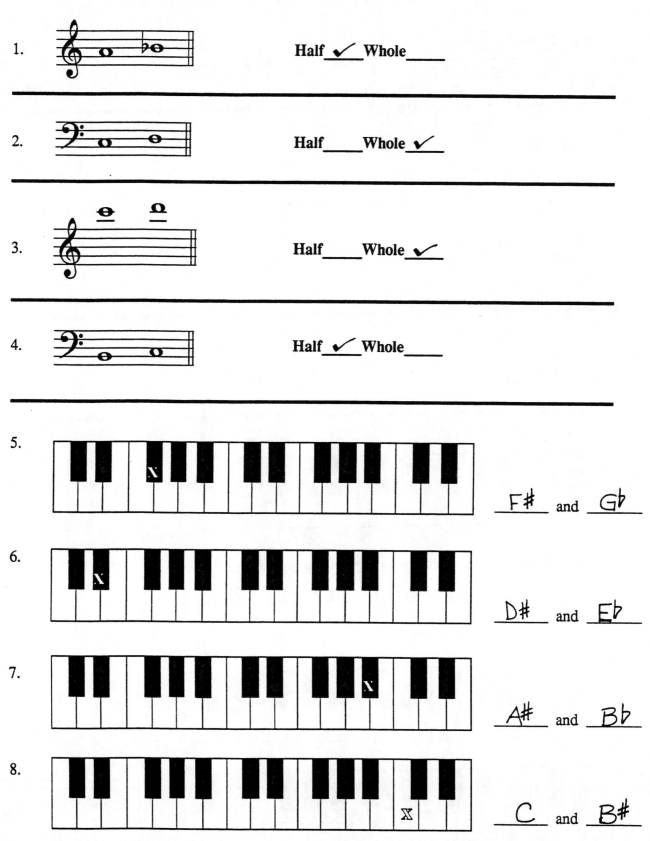

1.   Half ✔ Whole____

2.   Half____ Whole ✔

3.   Half____ Whole ✔

4.   Half ✔ Whole____

5.   ___F#___ and ___G♭___

6.   ___D#___ and ___E♭___

7.   ___A#___ and ___B♭___

8.   ___C___ and ___B#___

QUIZ-Chapter 5d-Accidentals

Name_____

Each of the following is either a half step or a whole step. Check the correct answer.

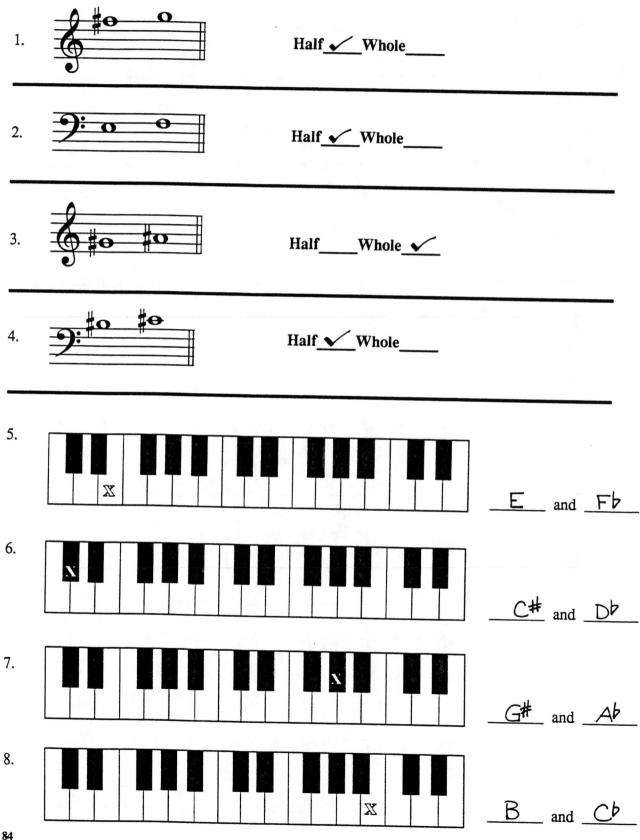

1.   Half ✓ Whole____

2.   Half ✓ Whole____

3.   Half____ Whole ✓

4.   Half ✓ Whole____

5.   E and F♭

6.   C♯ and D♭

7.   G♯ and A♭

8.   B and C♭

Name_____

Each of the following major scales has one incorrect note. Find the wrong note and place its number in the blank at the right.

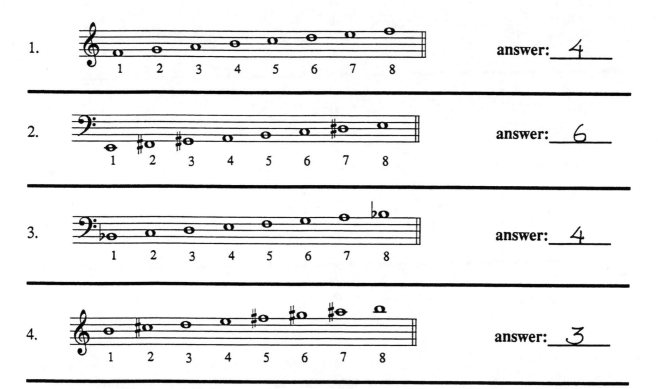

1. 1 2 3 4 5 6 7 8   answer: 4

2. 1 2 3 4 5 6 7 8   answer: 6

3. 1 2 3 4 5 6 7 8   answer: 4

4. 1 2 3 4 5 6 7 8   answer: 3

5. Write a major scale using the given note as tonic and adding accidentals as needed. Show the key signature for the scale on the staff beneath it.

Name_____

Each of the following major scales has one incorrect note. Find the wrong note and place its number in the blank at the right.

1. answer:___7___

2. answer:___7___

3. answer:___4___

4. answer:___7___

5. Write a major scale using the given note as tonic and adding accidentals as needed. Show the key signature for the scale on the staff beneath it.

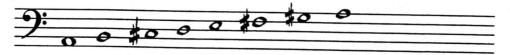

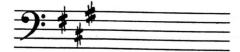

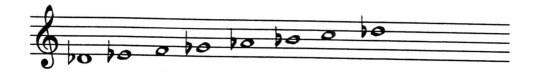

Name_____

Write the following major scales placing accidentals on notes as needed. Show the key signature for the scale in the space to the right.

1.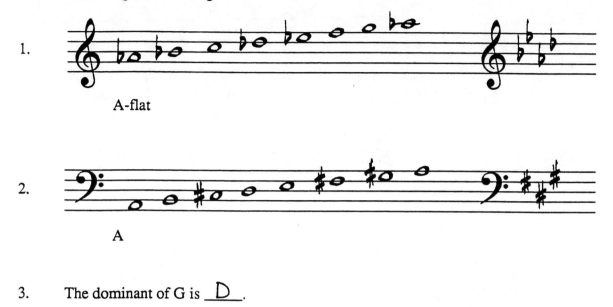

A-flat

2.

A

3. The dominant of G is __D__.

4. The dominant of E♭ is __B♭__.

The following melodies are in the key of C major.   Indicate the scale degree of each note using either solfeggio syllables (Do, Re, Mi, etc.) or numbers.

5.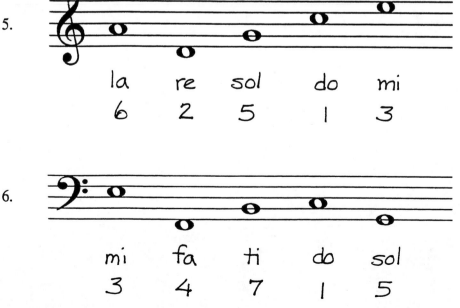

la	re	sol	do	mi
6	2	5	1	3

6.

mi	fa	ti	do	sol
3	4	7	1	5

Name_____

Write the following major scales placing accidentals on notes as needed. Show the key signature for the scale in the space to the right.

1.

G

2.

E

3.   The dominant of C# is G# .

4.   The dominant of A is E .

The following melodies are in the key of F major. Indicate the scale degree of each note using either solfeggio syllables (Do, Re, Mi, etc.) or numbers.

5.

fa   re   do   ti   sol
4   2   1   7   5

6.

mi   la   sol   fa   ti
3   6   5   4   7

QUIZ-Chapter 7a-Intervals

Name_____

In each group of five intervals all but one are the same size. Determine the different interval and place your answer in the blank at the right.

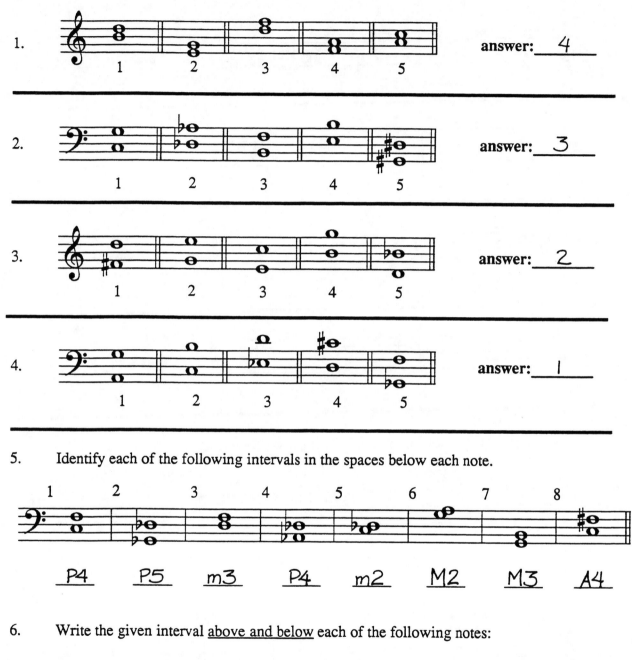

1. answer: __4__

2. answer: __3__

3. answer: __2__

4. answer: __1__

5. Identify each of the following intervals in the spaces below each note.

P4   P5   m3   P4   m2   M2   M3   A4

6. Write the given interval <u>above and below</u> each of the following notes:

P4   **M3**   **M6**   **P5**

QUIZ-Chapter 7b-Intervals

Name_____

In each group of five intervals all but one are the same size. Determine the different interval and place your answer in the blank at the right.

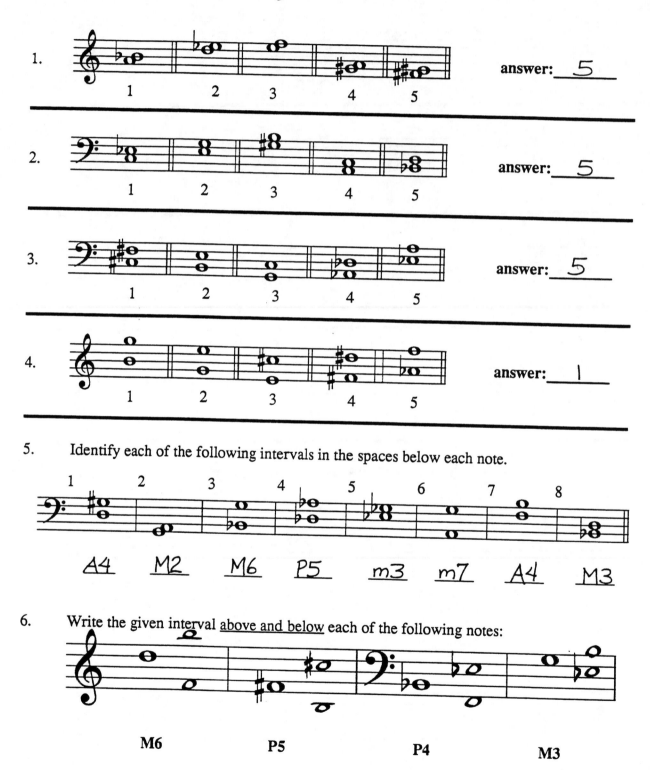

1.   1   2   3   4   5   answer: 5

2.   1   2   3   4   5   answer: 5

3.   1   2   3   4   5   answer: 5

4.   1   2   3   4   5   answer: 1

5.   Identify each of the following intervals in the spaces below each note.

1   2   3   4   5   6   7   8

A4   M2   M6   P5   m3   m7   A4   M3

6.   Write the given interval <u>above and below</u> each of the following notes:

M6   P5   P4   M3

Name_____

Identify the intervals between each tone in the melodies below (see example).

1.

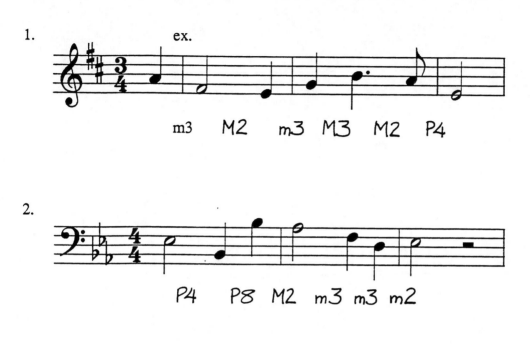

m3   M2   m3   M3   M2   P4

2.

P4   P8   M2   m3   m3   m2

3.   Write the given interval <u>above and below</u> each of the following notes:

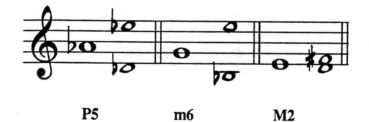

P5   **m6**   **M2**

4.   Define: Inversion of an interval

Raising the bottom tone of an interval by an octave. (Or lowering the top tone by an octave.)

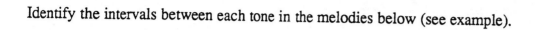

QUIZ-Chapter 7d-Intervals

Name_____

Identify the intervals between each tone in the melodies below (see example).

1.

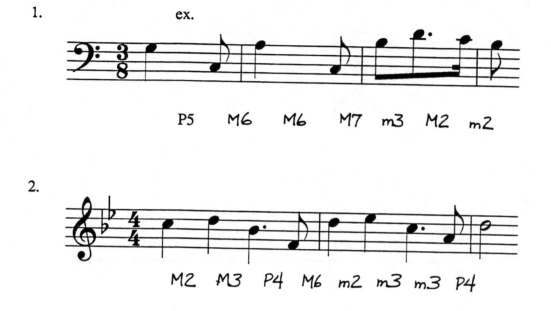

ex.

P5   M6   M6   M7   m3   M2   m2

2.

M2   M3   P4   M6   m2   m3   m3   P4

3.   Write the given interval <u>above and below</u> each of the following notes:

A4   M3   m7

4.   Define: Enharmonic interval

Two intervals that sound the same and are spelled differently are said to be enharmonic intervals.

QUIZ-Chapter 8a-Minor Keys

Name_____

Each of the following minor scales has one incorrect note. Find the wrong note and place its number in the blank at the right.

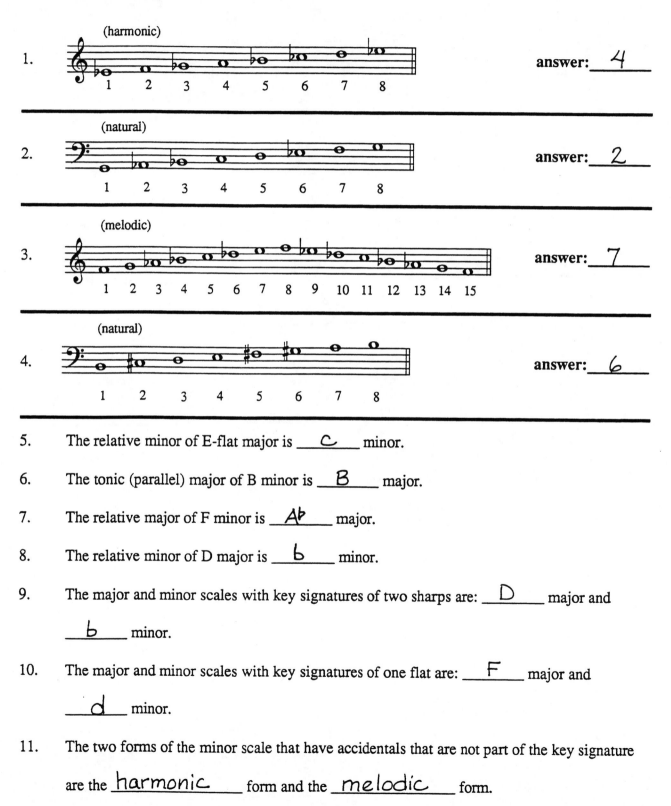

1. answer: __4__

2. answer: __2__

3. answer: __7__

4. answer: __6__

5. The relative minor of E-flat major is ___C___ minor.

6. The tonic (parallel) major of B minor is ___B___ major.

7. The relative major of F minor is ___Ab___ major.

8. The relative minor of D major is ___b___ minor.

9. The major and minor scales with key signatures of two sharps are: ___D___ major and ___b___ minor.

10. The major and minor scales with key signatures of one flat are: ___F___ major and ___d___ minor.

11. The two forms of the minor scale that have accidentals that are not part of the key signature are the __harmonic__ form and the __melodic__ form.

QUIZ-Chapter 8b-Minor Keys

Name_____

Each of the following minor scales has one incorrect note. Find the wrong note and place its number in the blank at the right.

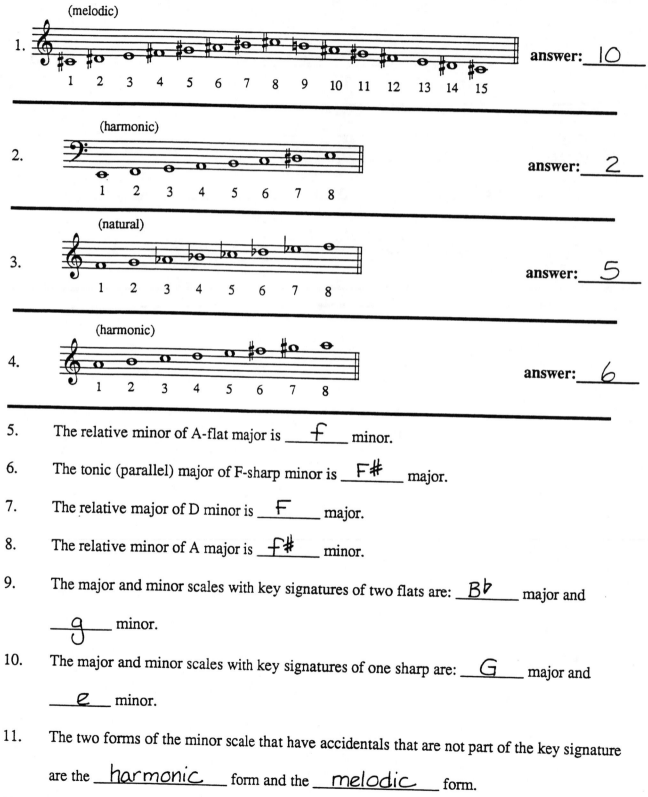

1. (melodic)   answer: __10__

2. (harmonic)   answer: __2__

3. (natural)   answer: __5__

4. (harmonic)   answer: __6__

5. The relative minor of A-flat major is ___f___ minor.

6. The tonic (parallel) major of F-sharp minor is ___F#___ major.

7. The relative major of D minor is ___F___ major.

8. The relative minor of A major is ___f#___ minor.

9. The major and minor scales with key signatures of two flats are: ___B♭___ major and ___g___ minor.

10. The major and minor scales with key signatures of one sharp are: ___G___ major and ___e___ minor.

11. The two forms of the minor scale that have accidentals that are not part of the key signature are the ___harmonic___ form and the ___melodic___ form.

Name_____

Write the following minor scales placing accidentals on notes as needed. Show the key signature for the scale in the space at the right.

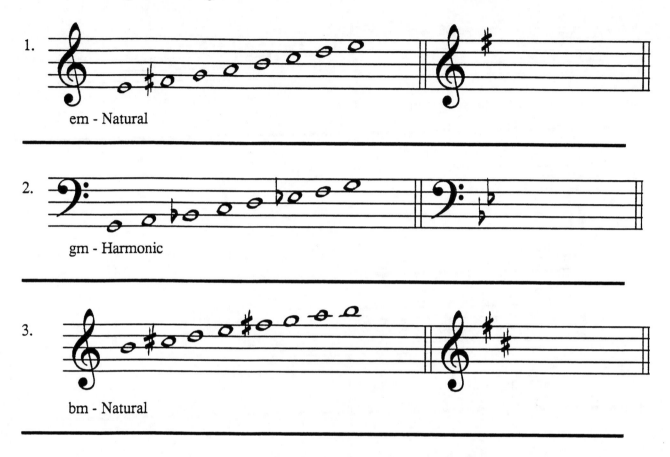

1.

em - Natural

2.

gm - Harmonic

3.

bm - Natural

4.   The interval between the tonic of a minor key and the tonic of its relative major is __m3__.

5.   The difference in number of sharps (or flats) between a minor key and its parallel major is

 __0__.

6.   Define: Circle of fifths

A clock face arrangement of the twelve pitches in the order of the number of accidentals in the key signature.

Name_____

Write the following minor scales placing accidentals on notes as needed. Show the key signature for the scale in the space at the right.

1.

cm - Melodic (ascending and descending)

2.

dm - Natural

3.

am - Harmonic

4. The interval between the tonic of a minor key and the tonic of its parallel major is __P1__.

5. The difference in number of sharps (or flats) between a minor key and its relative major is __3__.

6. Define: Circle of fifths

A clock face arrangement of the twelve pitches in the order of the number of accidentals in the key signature.

Name_____

1. Add one note to each of the following to make a major triad:

2. Add one note to each of the following to make a minor triad:

3. Write the popular music chord symbol above each of the following chords:

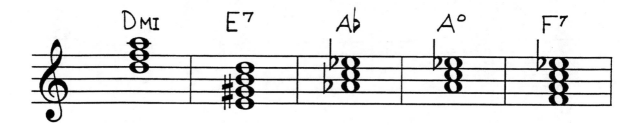

4. Write the chords requested below each popular chord symbol:

Name_____

1. Add one note to each of the following to make a major triad:

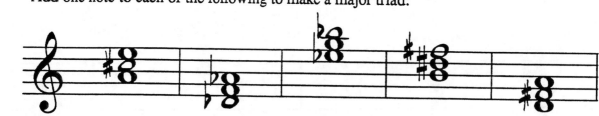

2. Add one note to each of the following to make a minor triad:

3. Write the popular music chord symbol above each of the following chords:

4. Write the chords requested below each popular chord symbol:

QUIZ-Chapter 9c-Chords

Name_____

Identify the expanded chords and write them in simplest position (see example).

Example: FMI   1. B♭MI   2. G⁷   3. D

4.   Form major triads on the following roots:

5.   Form minor seventh chords on the following roots:

Write the following triads in all inversions (see example).

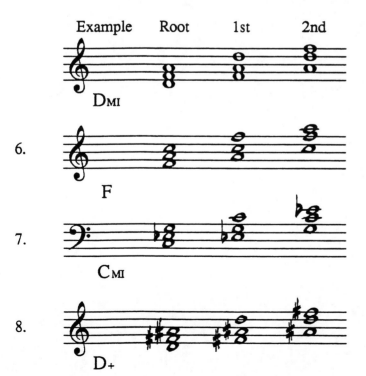

QUIZ-Chapter 9d-Chords

Name_____

Identify the expanded chords and write them in simplest position (see example).

Example: F MI   1. A   2. D⁷   3. C+

4.   Form major-minor seventh chords on the following roots (see example):

5.   Form minor triads on the following roots:

Write the following triads in all inversions (see example).

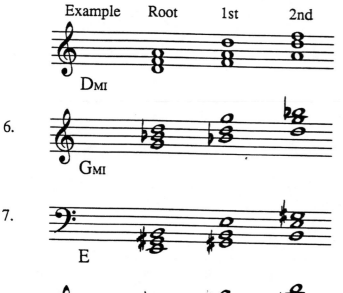

100

Name_____

1.   Write the three primary triads in each of the following keys. Remember to use the proper key signature.

F minor (harmonic form)

E-flat major

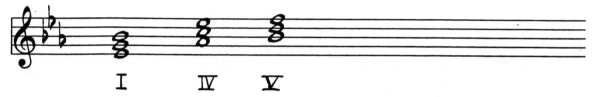

2.   Write the indicated chords on the staff below the melody. Do a roman numeral analysis of the chords in this song. Indicate all "circle progressions" by drawing a line between the chords.

QUIZ-Chapter 10b-Harmony

Name_____

1. Write the three primary triads in each of the following keys. Remember to use the proper key signature.

D minor (harmonic form)

        i   iv   V

A-flat major

        I   IV   V

2. Write the indicated chords on the staff below the melody. Do a roman numeral analysis of the chords in this song. Indicate all "circle progressions" by drawing a line between the chords.

102

Name_____

1. Write the three primary triads in each of the following keys. Remember to use the proper key signature.

B minor (harmonic form)

A major

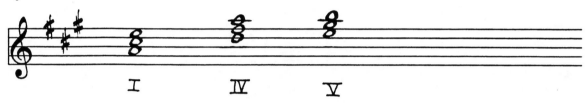

2. Write the indicated chords on the staff below the melody. Do a roman numeral analysis of the chords in this song. Indicate all "circle progressions" by drawing a line between the chords.

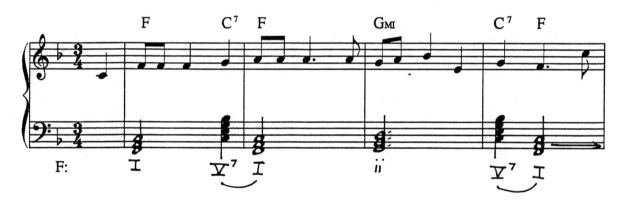

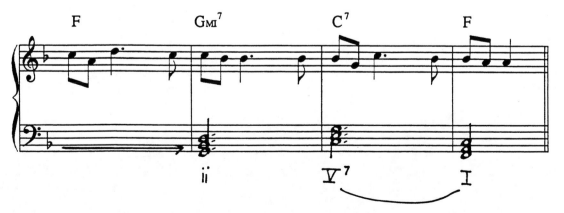

QUIZ-Chapter 10d-Harmony

Name_____

1.   Write the three primary triads in each of the following keys. Remember to use the proper key signature.

E major

C minor (harmonic form)

2.   Write the indicated chords on the staff below the melody. Do a roman numeral analysis of the chords in this song. Indicate all "circle progressions" by drawing a line between the chords.

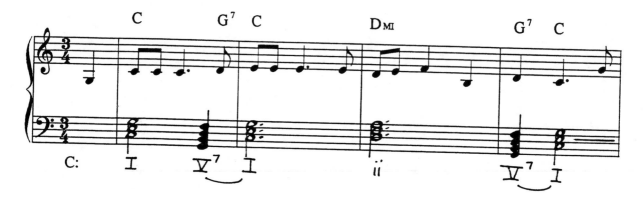

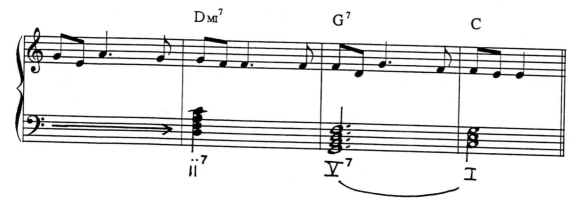

QUIZ-Chapter 11a-Harmonizing and Composing
Songs and Accompaniments

Name_____

1. Fill in the chords with the proper rhythm in the song "Barbara Allen" on the following page.

   Do a roman numeral analysis. (See the first chord for an example.)

2. Circle all nonharmonic notes in the melody of "Barbara Allen."

3. The harmonic cadence in measure four (A) is a(n) ____half____ cadence.

4. The harmonic cadence in the final measure (D) is a(n) __authentic__ cadence.

5. The harmonic rhythm throughout the song is _dotted half notes_ (note value) except

   measure _____7_____ which is _quarter note_ (note value).

"Barbara Allen"

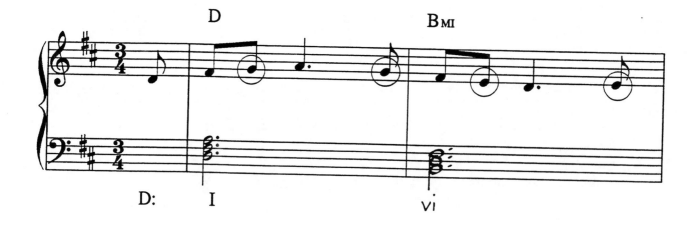

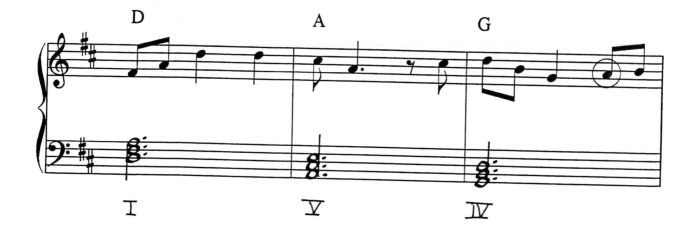

QUIZ-Chapter 11b-Harmonizing and Composing
Songs and Accompaniments

Name_____

1. Fill in the chords with the proper rhythm in the song "Barbara Allen" on the following page.

    Do a roman numeral analysis. (See the first chord for an example.)

2. Circle all nonharmonic notes in the melody of "Barbara Allen."

3. The harmonic cadence in measure four (F) is a(n) ___half___ cadence.

4. The harmonic cadence in the final measure (B-flat) is a(n) ___authentic___ cadence.

5. The harmonic rhythm throughout the song is ___dotted half note___ (note value) except

    measure ___7___ which is ___quarter note___ (note value).

"Barbara Allen"

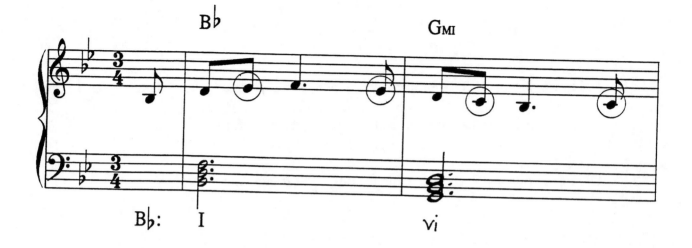

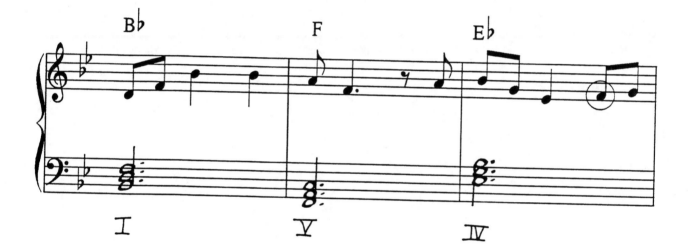

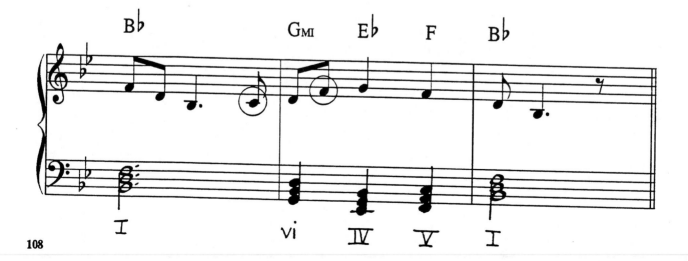

Name_____

1.   Fill in the chords with the proper rhythm in the song "Simple Gifts" on the following page.

Do a roman numeral analysis. (See the first chord for an example.)

2.   Circle all nonharmonic notes in the melody of "Simple Gifts."

3.   Mark the end of the first phrase. What is the harmonic cadence here?

4.   Mark the end of the second phrase. What is the harmonic cadence here?

5.   Graph the contour of the first phrase above the melody.

"Simple Gifts"

Name_____

1.   Fill in the chords with the proper rhythm in the song "Simple Gifts" on the following page.

          Do a roman numeral analysis. (See the first chord for an example.)

2.   Circle all nonharmonic notes in the melody of "Simple Gifts."

3.   Mark the end of the first phrase. What is the harmonic cadence here?

4.   Mark the end of the second phrase. What is the harmonic cadence here?

5.   Graph the contour of the second phrase above the melody.

"Simple Gifts"

A: I

Half cadence

V   I

Plagal cadence

V   I   IV   I

Final Examinations

If this test is to be scored by machine, <u>do NOT write in or mark the pamphlet in any way</u>. Your answers are to be recorded on the form that has been supplied. Be sure that the number of your answer corresponds with the number of the item in each case. An answer may be changed if the original response is erased thoroughly. Try not to spend too much time on any one item.

1. In which case is the A major scale correctly notated?

2. The <u>parallel</u> (tonic) minor of E♭ major has as its key signature:

    (1) three flats   (2) five flats   (3) four sharps

    (4) one sharp   (5) none of these

3. The B harmonic minor scale has as its <u>seventh scale degree</u>:

    (1) C♯   (2) A   (3) F♯   (4) B♭   (5) A♯

4. The G♯ melodic minor scale (ascending form) has as its sixth scale degree:

    (1) B   (2) E   (3) E♯   (4) C♯   (5) B♯

5. The triad below is:

    (1) major
    (2) minor
    (3) diminished
    (4) augmented

6. The triad below is:

    (1) major
    (2) minor
    (3) diminished
    (4) augmented

7. In which case is the chord <u>incorrectly</u> spelled?

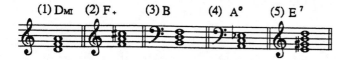

(1) D$_{MI}$ (2) F$_+$ (3) B   (4) A$^°$ (5) E^7

8. Select the correct time signature for the measure below.

(1) $\frac{6}{8}$ (2) $\frac{3}{4}$ (3) ¢   (4) $\frac{12}{8}$ (5) $\frac{4}{2}$

9. Which of the following sequences of chords form a <u>circle progression</u>?

(1)   (2)   (3)

F: G: C:

10. Which measure of the following melody contains an error in rhythmic notation?

(1)   (2)   (3)   (4)   (5)

11. Which measure of the following melody contains an error in rhythmic notation?

(1)   (2)   (3)   (4)

12. In which case is the F♯ melodic minor scale correctly notated?

(1)

(2)

(3)

13. In which case are the primary chords correctly notated?

F: D: c:

14. In which case is the B natural minor scale correctly notated?

15. The parallel (tonic) major of B minor has as its key signature:

        (1) two sharps   (2) two flats   (3) five sharps

        (4) five flats   (5) none of these

16. The second scale degree of E major is:

    (1) F♯   (2) D   (3) D♯   (4) F   (5) D♭

17. Which chord has an incorrect roman numeral analysis?

G: V⁷   B♭: vii°   E♭: ii   b: ii°

18. A perfect fifth <u>below</u> F is:

    (1) C   (2) B   (3) C♯   (4) B♭   (5) C♭

19. A minor sixth <u>above</u> G is:

    (1) D♯   (2) E   (3) E♭   (4) B♭   (5) E♯

20. The interval from the fourth scale degree up to the second scale degree of a major scale is:

(1) a perfect fourth (2) a minor seventh (3) a major sixth

(4) a major third (5) a minor sixth

21. The interval from the third to the fifth of an augmented triad is:

(1) an augmented third (2) an augmented fifth (3) a major third

(4) a minor sixth (5) none of these

22. The augmented triad with E as its fifth has as its root:

(1) A (2) A# (3) G# (4) C (5) A♭

23. In which case is the chord incorrectly spelled?

(1) A$_{MI}^{7}$ (2) E^{7} (3) G$_{+}$ (4) G$_{MI}^{7}$ (5) C#°

24. The major triad with A♭ as its third has as its fifth:

(1) C♭ (2) C (3) B (4) F♭ (5) F

25. The harmonic minor scale which has D as its sixth scale degree is:

(1) G minor (2) F minor (3) B minor

(4) B♭ minor (5) F# minor

26. In the B harmonic minor scale the dominant is:

(1) F# (2) E (3) F (4) E# (5) G

27. The interval is a(n):

(1) augmented fourth (2) diminished fourth (3) perfect fourth

(4) minor fourth (5) none of these

28. The triad below is:

(1) major
(2) minor
(3) diminished
(4) augmented

29. In which case is the following melodic motive (in B♭ minor) correctly transposed to another key?

30. A  note is equal to (1, 2, 3, 4, 5)  rests.

31. Which chord has an incorrect roman numeral analysis?

F: vi   A: iii   e: vii°   E♭: IV

32. Which measure of the following melody contains an error in rhythmic notation?

33. Which measure of the following melody contains an error in rhythmic notation?

34. The <u>major</u> scale which has a signature of four sharps is:

(1) A   (2) E   (3) A♯   (4) B   (5) D♯

35. The <u>minor</u> scale with a signature of five flats is:

(1) B♭   (2) A♭   (3) G♭   (4) C♭   (5) D♭

36. The third scale degree of G melodic minor (ascending form) is:

(1) E   (2) B♭   (3) E♭   (4) B   (5) E♯

37. An augmented fourth <u>below</u> B is:

(1) F   (2) E   (3) E♭   (4) F♭   (5) F♯

38. A minor third <u>above</u> B♯ is:

(1) D   (2) D♯   (3) G♯   (4) E♭   (5) D♭

39. The two notes below are the third and fifth of an augmented triad. What is the root?

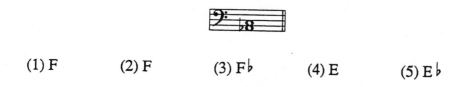

(1) F   (2) F   (3) F♭   (4) E   (5) E♭

40. The two notes below are the root and fifth of a minor triad. What is the third?

(1) E   (2) F♯   (3) E♭   (4) F   (5) F♭

41. In which case is the following melodic motive (in D major) correctly transposed to another major key?

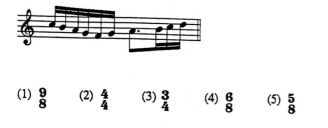

42. Select the correct time signature for the measure below.

(1) $\frac{9}{8}$ (2) $\frac{4}{4}$ (3) $\frac{3}{4}$ (4) $\frac{6}{8}$ (5) $\frac{5}{8}$

43. In which case is the B♭ major scale correctly notated?

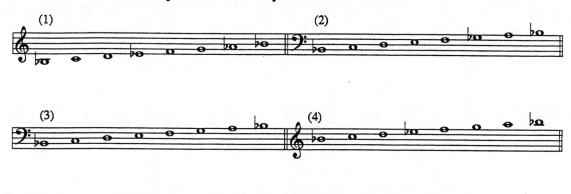

44. The key signature of the major scale that is <u>enharmonic</u> with B major is:

(1) five sharps   (2) two flats   (3) seven sharps

(4) seven flats   (5) two sharps

45. In which case are the <u>primary chords</u> correctly notated?

46. In which case is the key signature of C♯ minor correctly notated?

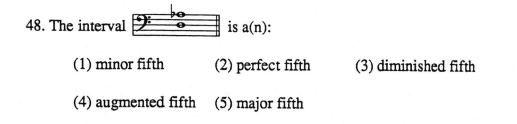

47. The interval  is a(n):

(1) major sixth   (2) minor sixth   (3) augmented sixth

(4) minor seventh   (5) diminished seventh

48. The interval  is a(n):

(1) minor fifth   (2) perfect fifth   (3) diminished fifth

(4) augmented fifth   (5) major fifth

49. In which case is the following melodic motive (in F# minor) correctly transposed to another minor key?

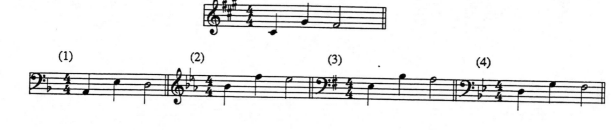

(1)   (2)   (3)   (4)

50. A  rest is equal to (1, 2, 3, 4, 5) notes.

51. Select the correct time signature for the measure below.

(1) $\frac{9}{8}$ (2) $\frac{6}{8}$ (3) $\frac{5}{8}$ (4) $\frac{3}{4}$ (5) $\frac{5}{4}$

52. Which measure of the following melody contains an error in rhythmic notation?

(1)   (2)   (3)   (4)   (5)

53. The <u>relative</u> minor of B major is:

    (1) F minor   (2) G minor   (3) A♭ minor

    (4) D minor   (5) G# minor

54. The <u>relative</u> major of C minor is:

    (1) G major   (2) C# major   (3) E major

    (4) C major   (5) E♭ major

55. A minor seventh <u>below</u> F# is:

    (1) A♭   (2) G   (3) G♭   (4) G#   (5) none of these

56. The interval between the sixth scale degree and the seventh scale degree of a harmonic minor scale is:

       (1) a whole step   (2) a major third   (3) an augmented second

       (4) a minor third   (5) none of these

57. The two notes below are part of a major triad. What other note is needed?

       (1) B   (2) B♭   (3) C   (4) C♭   (5) none of these

58. The diminished triad with G as its third has as its fifth:

       (1) B   (2) A♯   (3) B♯   (4) B♭   (5) D♭

59. In which case is the following melodic motive (in C minor) correctly transposed to another minor key?

60. Select the correct time signature for the measure below.

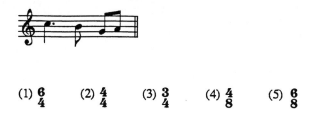

       (1) $\frac{6}{4}$ (2) $\frac{4}{4}$ (3) $\frac{3}{4}$ (4) $\frac{4}{8}$ (5) $\frac{6}{8}$

MUSIC FUNDAMENTALS EXAMINATION
(FORM B)

If this test is to be scored by machine, <u>do NOT write in or mark the pamphlet in any way</u>. Your answers are to be recorded on the form that has been supplied. Be sure that the number of your answer corresponds with the number of the item in each case. An answer may be changed if the original response is erased thoroughly. Try not to spend too much time on any one item.

1. In which case is the following melodic motive (in C minor) correctly transposed to another minor key?

2. The <u>relative</u> minor of B major is:

   (1) F minor   (2) G minor   (3) A♭ minor

   (4) D minor   (5) G♯ minor

3. The <u>relative</u> major of C minor is:

   (1) G major   (2) C♯ major   (3) E major

   (4) C major   (5) E♭ major

4. The interval between the sixth scale degree and the seventh scale degree of a harmonic minor scale is:

   (1) a whole step   (2) a major third   (3) an augmented second

   (4) a minor third   (5) none of these

5. The two notes below are part of a major triad. What other note is needed?

   (1) B   (2) B♭   (3) C   (4) C♭   (5) none of these

6. Which measure of the following melody contains an error in rhythmic notation?

7. In which case is the chord <u>incorrectly</u> spelled?

8. A minor seventh <u>below</u> F♯ is:

    (1) A♭   (2) G   (3) G♭   (4) G♯   (5) none of these

9. Which of the following sequences of chords form a <u>circle progression</u>?

10. Select the correct time signature for the measure below.

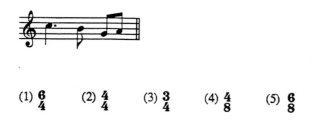

    (1) $\frac{6}{4}$ (2) $\frac{4}{4}$ (3) $\frac{3}{4}$ (4) $\frac{4}{8}$ (5) $\frac{6}{8}$

11. The two notes below are the third and fifth of an augmented triad. What is the root?

    (1) F♯   (2) F   (3) F♭   (4) E   (5) E♭

12. In which case is the following melodic motive (in D major) correctly transposed to another major key?

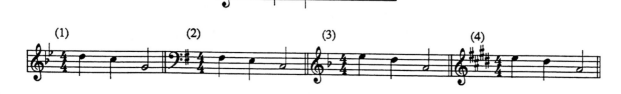

126

13. In which case are the <u>primary chords</u> correctly notated?

14. Select the correct time signature for the measure below.

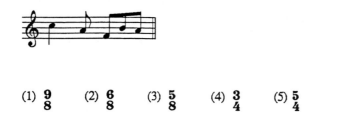

(1) $\frac{9}{8}$ (2) $\frac{6}{8}$ (3) $\frac{5}{8}$ (4) $\frac{3}{4}$ (5) $\frac{5}{4}$

15. In which case is the key signature of C$\sharp$ minor correctly notated?

16. The interval  is a(n):

(1) major sixth   (2) minor sixth   (3) augmented sixth

(4) minor seventh   (5) diminished seventh

17. Which chord has an incorrect roman numeral analysis?

G: V^7 B$\flat$: vii°   E$\flat$: ii   b: ii°

18. The diminished triad with G as its third has as its fifth:

(1) B   (2) A$\sharp$ (3) B$\sharp$ (4) B$\flat$ (5) D$\flat$

19. The interval is a(n):

(1) minor fifth   (2) perfect fifth   (3) diminished fifth

(4) augmented fifth   (5) major fifth

20. A ≡ rest is equal to (1, 2, 3, 4, 5) ≡ notes.

21. The interval from the third to the fifth of an augmented triad is:

    (1) an augmented third   (2) an augmented fifth   (3) a major third

    (4) a minor sixth   (5) none of these

22. The <u>harmonic</u> minor scale which has D as its sixth scale degree is:

    (1) G minor   (2) F minor   (3) B minor

    (4) B♭ minor   (5) F♯ minor

23. In which case is the chord <u>incorrectly</u> spelled?

24. In which case is the following melodic motive (in F♯ minor) correctly transposed to another minor key?

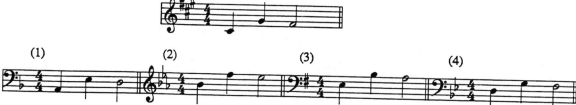

25. The augmented triad with E as its fifth has as its root:

    (1) A   (2) A♯   (3) G♯   (4) C   (5) A♭

26. The <u>minor</u> scale with a signature of five flats is:

    (1) B♭   (2) A♭   (3) G♭   (4) C♭   (5) D♭

27. The interval [♪] is a(n):

    (1) augmented fourth   (2) diminished fourth   (3) perfect fourth

    (4) minor fourth   (5) none of these

28. A minor third <u>above</u> B♯ is:

(1) D   (2) D♯   (3) G♯   (4) E♭   (5) D♭

29. The third scale degree of G melodic minor (ascending form) is:

(1) E   (2) B♭   (3) E♭   (4) B   (5) E♯

30. The <u>major</u> scale which has a signature of four sharps is:

(1) A   (2) E   (3) A♯   (4) B   (5) D♯

31. Which chord has an incorrect roman numeral analysis?

F: vi   A: iii   e: vii°   E♭: IV

32. Which measure of the following melody contains an error in rhythmic notation?

33. The two notes below are the root and fifth of a minor triad. What is the third?

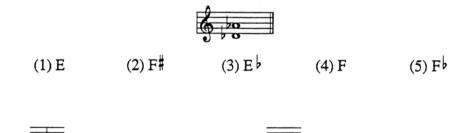

(1) E   (2) F♯   (3) E♭   (4) F   (5) F♭

34. A 𝅘𝅥𝅮 note is equal to (1, 2, 3, 4, 5) 𝄾 rests.

35. In the B harmonic minor scale the <u>dominant</u> is:

(1) F♯   (2) E   (3) F   (4) E♯   (5) G

36. In which case is the following melodic motive (in B♭ minor) correctly transposed to another key?

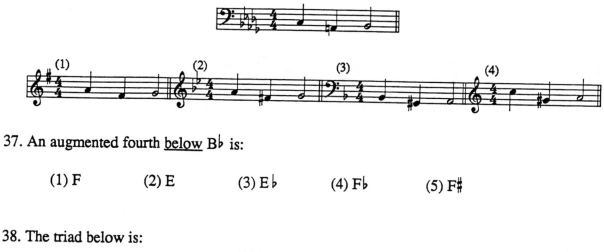

37. An augmented fourth below B♭ is:

    (1) F   (2) E   (3) E♭   (4) F♭   (5) F♯

38. The triad below is:

    (1) major
    (2) minor
    (3) diminished
    (4) augmented

39. Which measure of the following melody contains an error in rhythmic notation?

40. Which measure of the following melody contains an error in rhythmic notation?

41. In which case is the F♯ melodic minor scale correctly notated?

42. In which case is the B♭ major scale correctly notated?

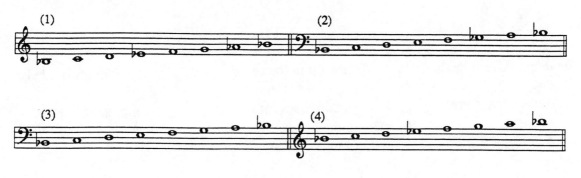

43. The key signature of the major scale that is <u>enharmonic</u> with B major is:

    (1) five sharps   (2) two flats   (3) seven sharps

    (4) seven flats   (5) two sharps

44. Select the correct time signature for the measure below.

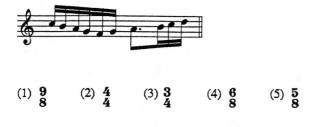

  (1) $\frac{9}{8}$ (2) $\frac{4}{4}$ (3) $\frac{3}{4}$ (4) $\frac{6}{8}$ (5) $\frac{5}{8}$

45. In which case are the <u>primary chords</u> correctly notated?

46. The parallel (tonic) major of B minor has as its key signature:

    (1) two sharps   (2) two flats   (3) five sharps

    (4) five flats   (5) none of these

47. The second scale degree of E major is:

    (1) F♯   (2) D   (3) D♯   (4) F   (5) D♭

48. A minor sixth <u>above</u> G is:

    (1) D♯   (2) E   (3) E♭   (4) B♭   (5) E♯

49. The major triad with A♭ as its third has as its fifth:

    (1) C♭   (2) C   (3) B   (4) F♭   (5) F

50. The interval from the fourth scale degree <u>up</u> to the second scale degree of a major scale is:

    (1) a perfect fourth   (2) a minor seventh   (3) a major sixth

    (4) a major third   (5) a minor sixth

51. In which case is the B natural minor scale correctly notated?

52. The triad below is:

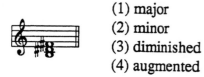

    (1) major
    (2) minor
    (3) diminished
    (4) augmented

53. The <u>parallel</u> (tonic) minor of E♭ major has as its key signature:

    (1) three flats   (2) five flats   (3) four sharps

    (4) one sharp   (5) none of these

54. The B harmonic minor scale has as its <u>seventh scale degree</u>:

    (1) C♯   (2) A   (3) F♯   (4) B♭   (5) A♯

55. Select the correct time signature for the measure below.

    (1) $\frac{6}{8}$ (2) $\frac{3}{4}$ (3) ¢   (4) $\frac{12}{8}$ (5) $\frac{4}{2}$

56. The G♯ melodic minor scale (ascending form) has as its <u>sixth scale degree:</u>

    (1) B   (2) E   (3) E♯   (4) C♯   (5) B♯

57. The triad below is:

                                                      (1) major
                                                      (2) minor
                                                      (3) diminished
                                                      (4) augmented

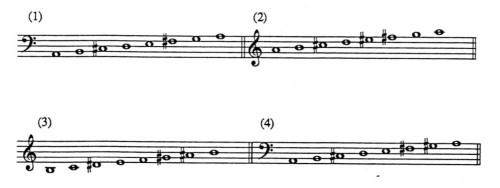

58. A perfect fifth <u>below</u> F is:

    (1) C   (2) B   (3) C♯   (4) B♭   (5) C♭

59. In which case is the A major scale correctly notated?

60. Which measure of the following melody contains an error in rhythmic notation?

Key for Final Examinations

Key for Music Fundamentals Examination
(Forms A and B)

1.	4		31.	1
2.	5		32.	3
3.	5		33.	5
4.	3		34.	2
5.	4		35.	1
6.	1		36.	2
7.	3		37.	4
8.	4		38.	2
9.	1		39.	3
10.	3		40.	5
11.	3		41.	3
12.	3		42.	4
13.	2		43.	4
14.	2		44.	4
15.	3		45.	1
16.	1		46.	3
17.	2		47.	1
18.	4		48.	3
19.	3		49.	1
20.	3		50.	3
21.	3		51.	2
22.	5		52.	1
23.	2		53.	5
24.	1		54.	5
25.	5		55.	4
26.	1		56.	3
27.	1		57.	4
28.	2		58.	4
29.	2		59.	4
30.	2		60.	3

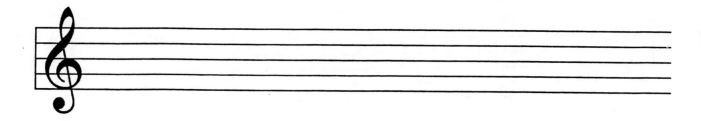

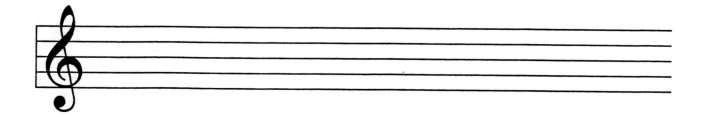

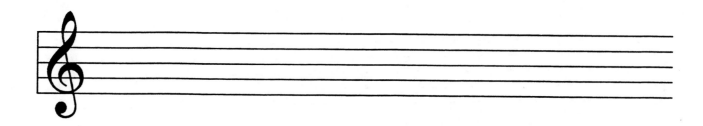

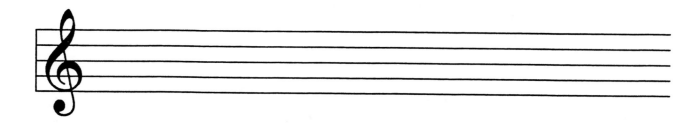

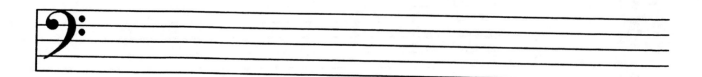

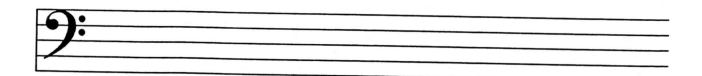

Relative Note and Rest Values

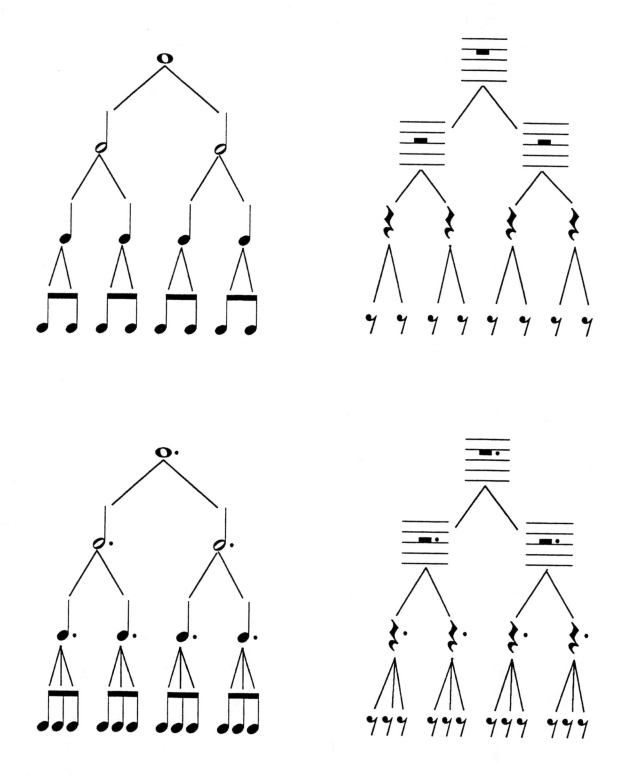

Name	Note	Rest	Equivalents

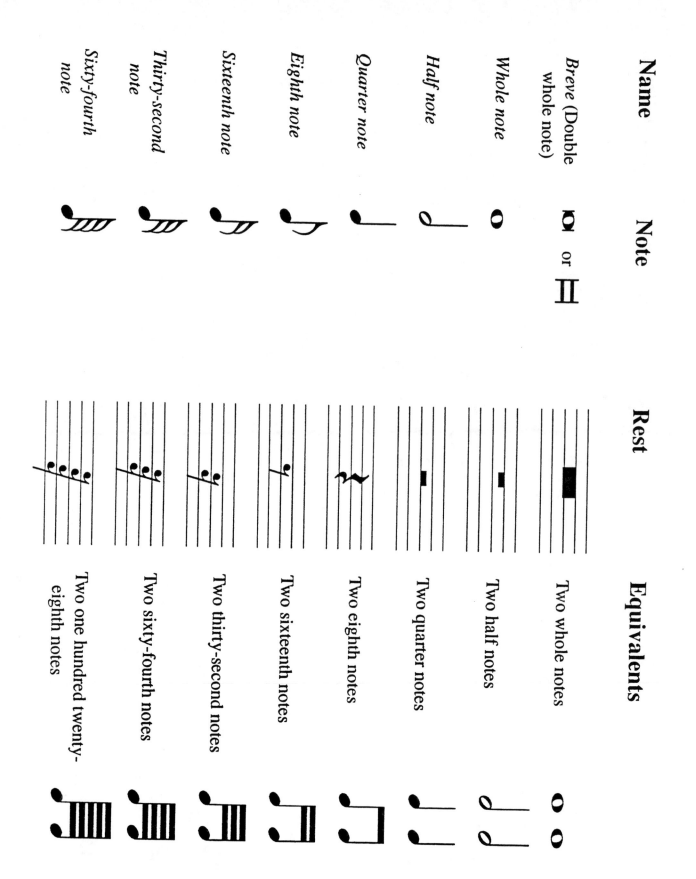

Breve (Double whole note)

Whole note

Half note

Quarter note

Eighth note

Sixteenth note

Thirty-second note

Sixty-fourth note

Two whole notes

Two half notes

Two quarter notes

Two eighth notes

Two sixteenth notes

Two thirty-second notes

Two sixty-fourth notes

Two one hundred twenty-eighth notes

1. ♯

2.  𝄞

3. ♮

4.  𝄢

5. 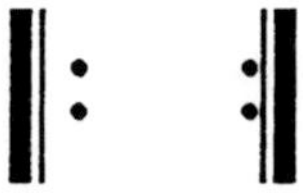 𝄆   𝄇

6. ♭

7. 𝄾

8. 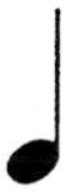 ♩

9.  ♪

10. 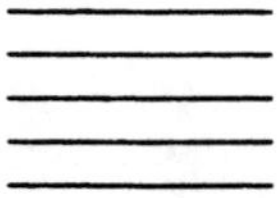 (staff lines)

11. *p*

12.  𝄴

13. 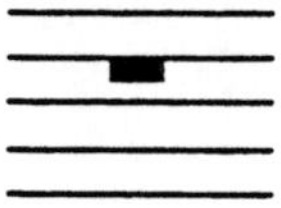 (whole rest)

14.  𝄼

15.  𝄵

16.  ♪

17.  (half rest)

18.  𝄿

19. 𝅝

20. 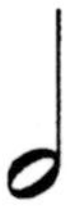 𝅗𝅥

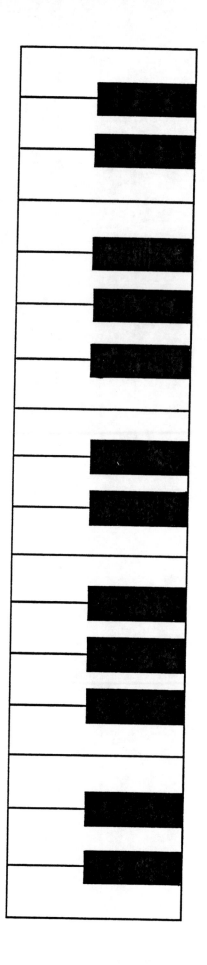

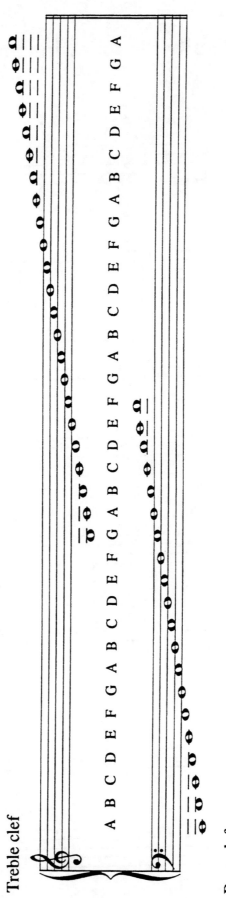

Identify the following notes:

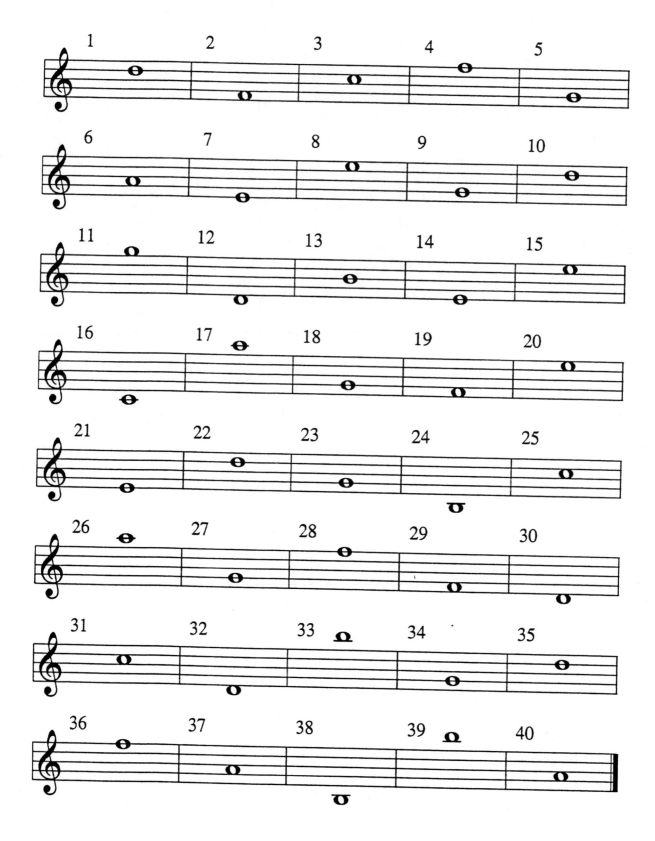

Identify the following notes:

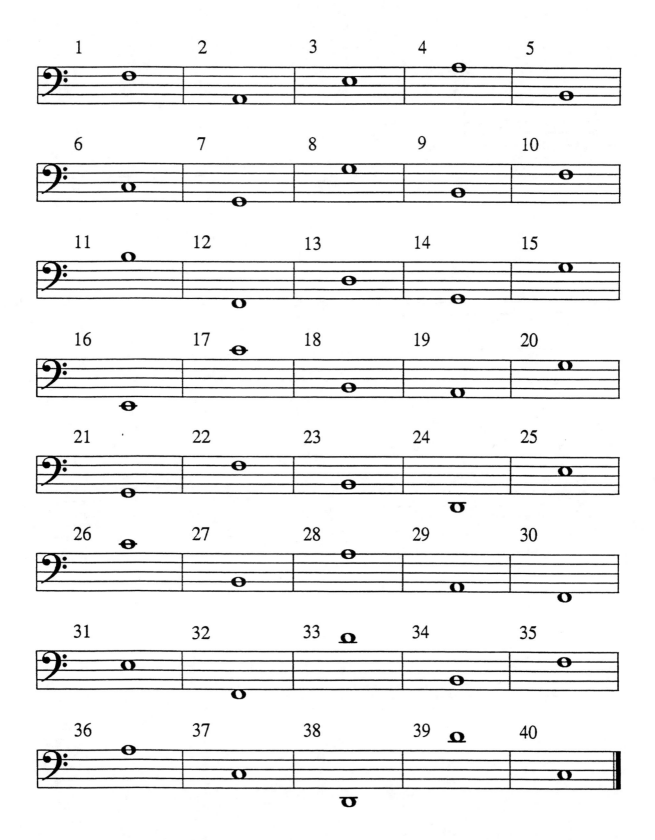

Grand Staff Note Identification

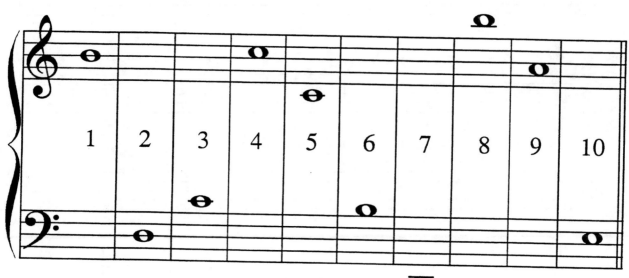

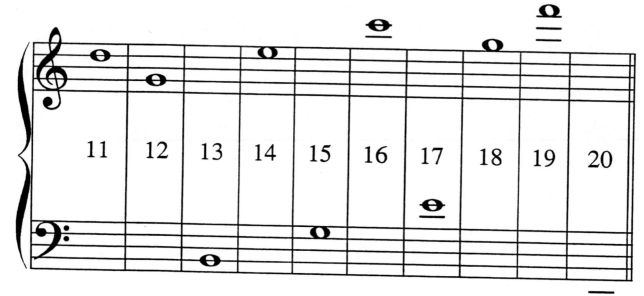

Major or Minor Scales

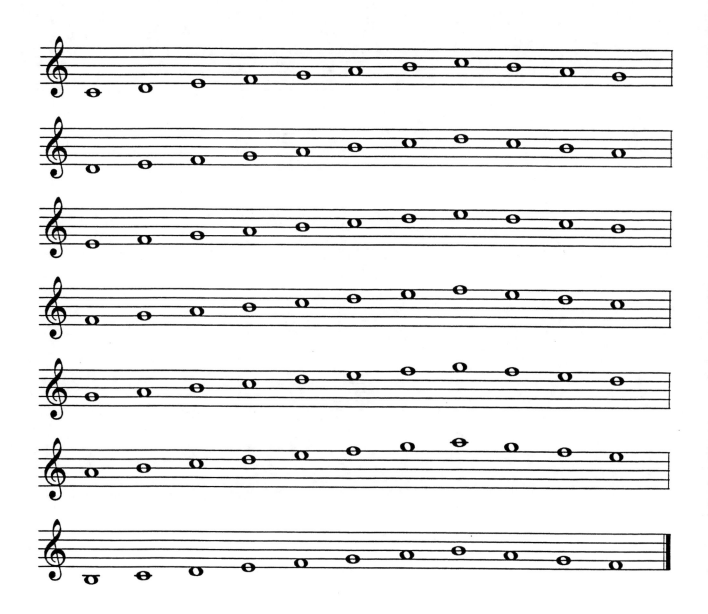

Major or Minor Scales

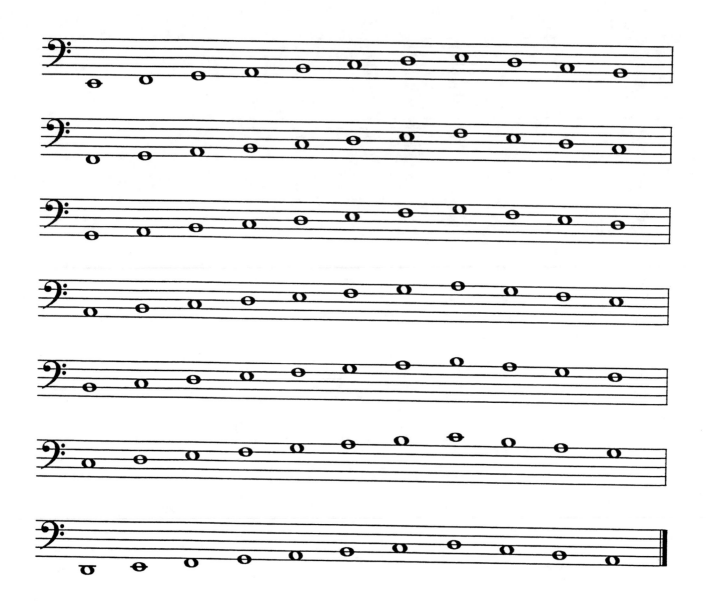

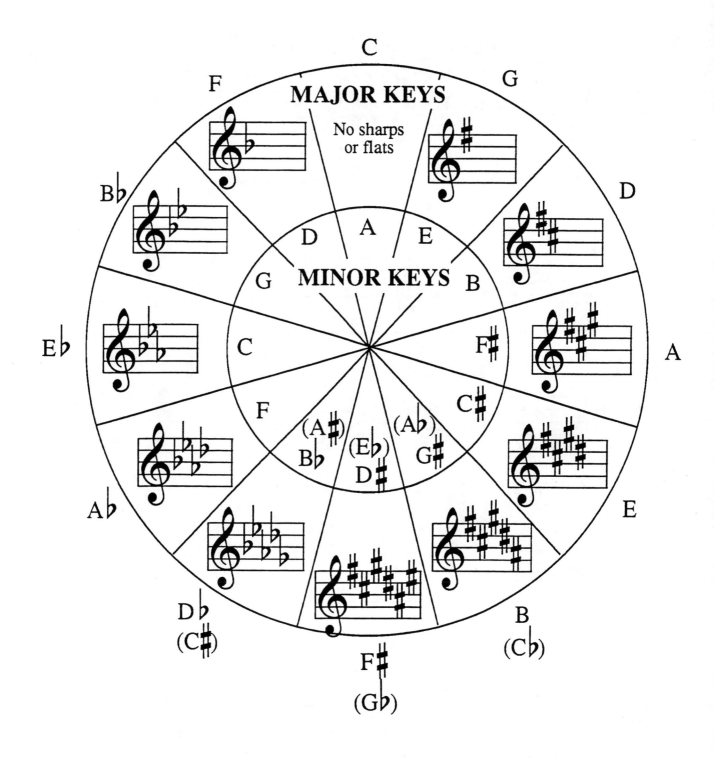

Key Signatures

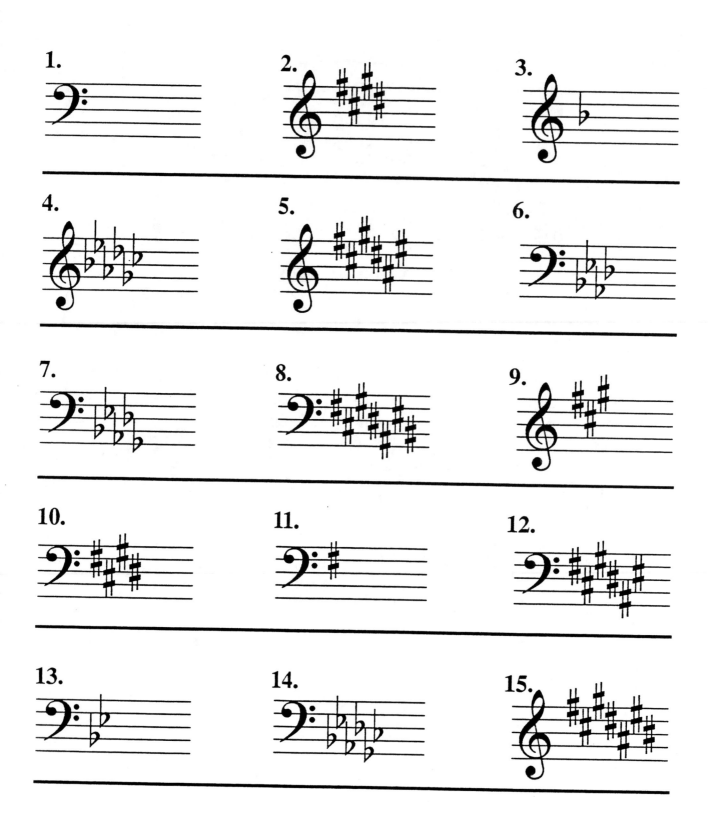

Key Signatures

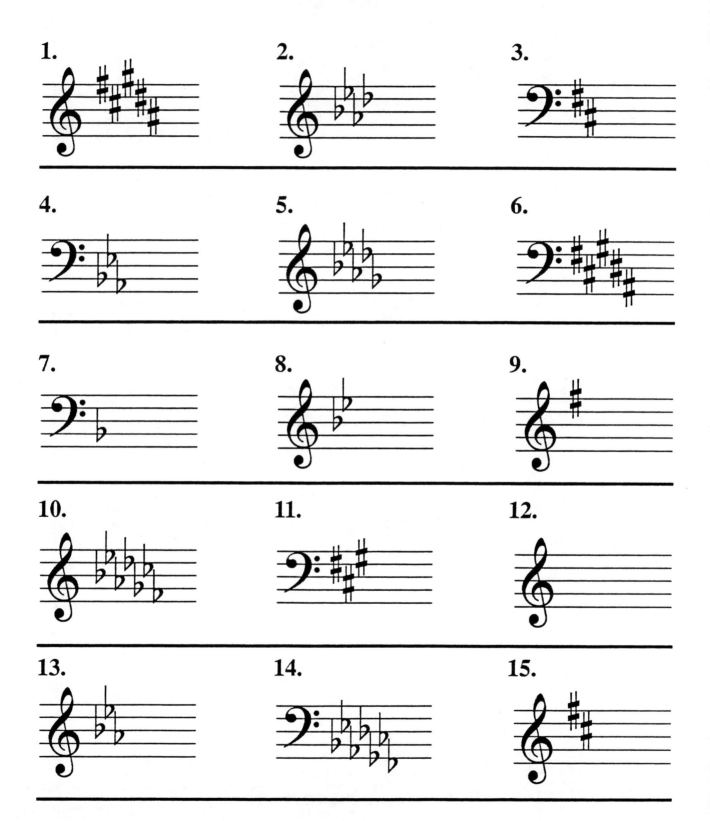

Intervals

Write each of the intervals above and below the following notes:

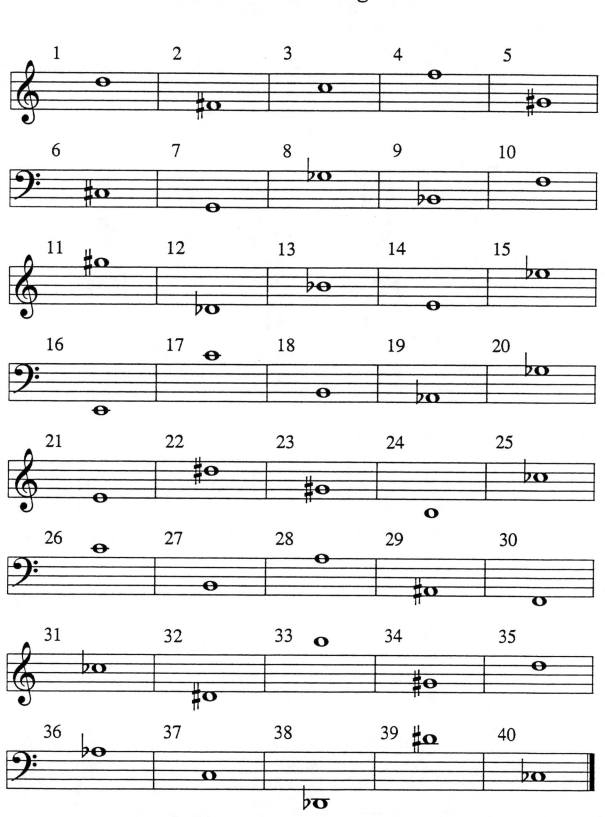

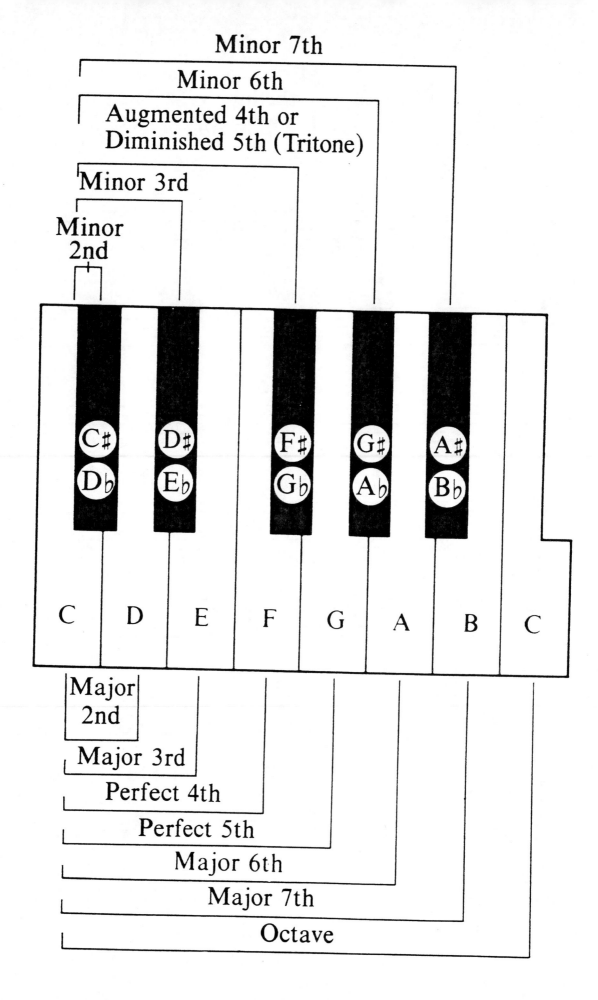

Major and Minor Triads

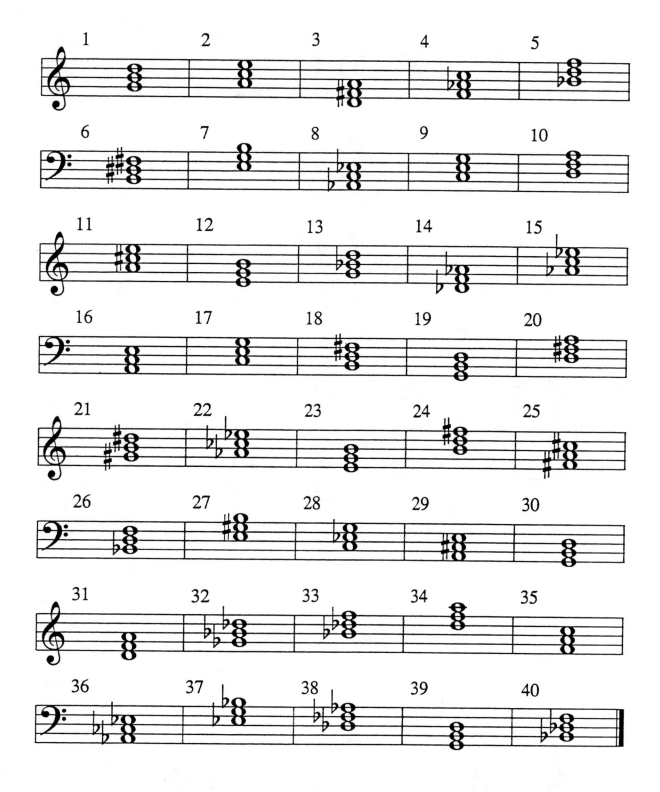

Supply the remaining pitch to complete a major triad.
Now supply a pitch which would create a minor triad.

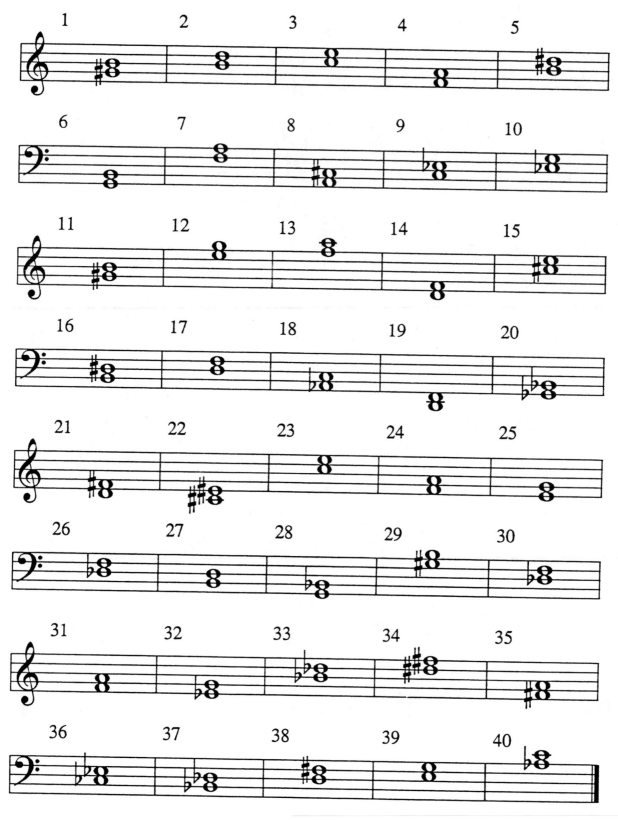

Keys for Assignments

Assignments

Chapter 1 (p. 7)–Assignment 1: Note values

The two groups of notes and rests in each following question contain different numbers of beats. Add up the number of quarter-note beats in each group, identify the shorter group in the blank at the right, and give the number of beats it is shorter than the longer group. (See example.)

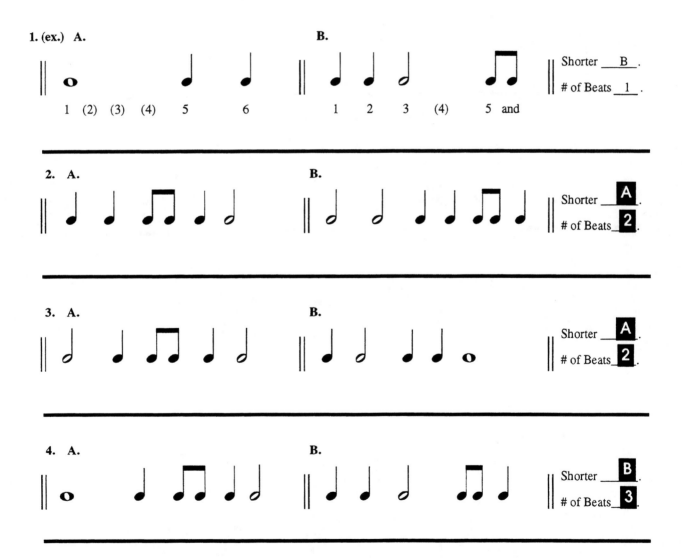

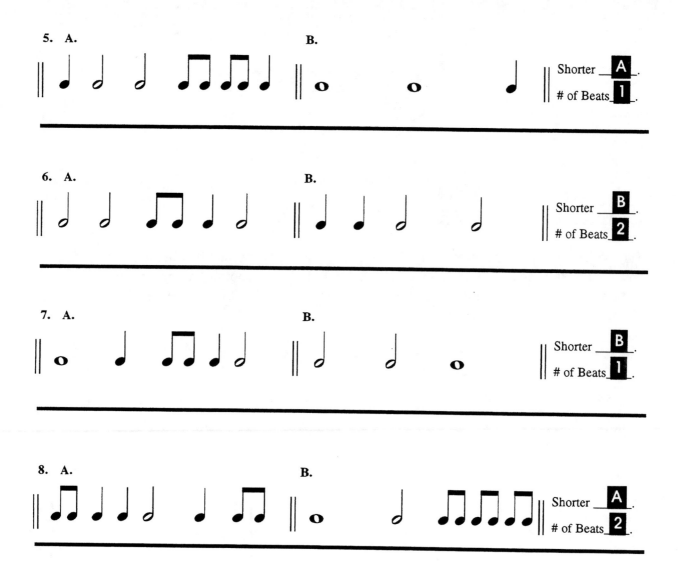

Chapter 1 (p. 9)–Assignment 2a:
Ties and dots

Rewrite the following rhythms replacing all ties:

Chapter 1 (p. 9)–Assignment 2b: Ties and dots

Rewrite the following rhythms replacing all dotted notes with tied notes:

Chapter 1 (p. 12)–Assignment 3a:
Rests in simple time

Replace each note with the equivalent rest:

Chapter 1 (p. 12)–Assignment 3b: Rests in compound time

Replace each note with the equivalent rest:

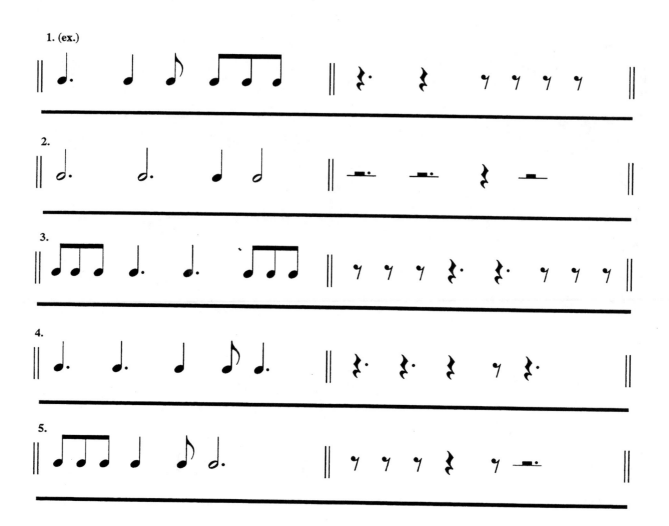

Chapter 2 (p. 21)–Assignment 4a:
Names of notes in the treble staff

Write the names of each of the following notes in the blanks below:

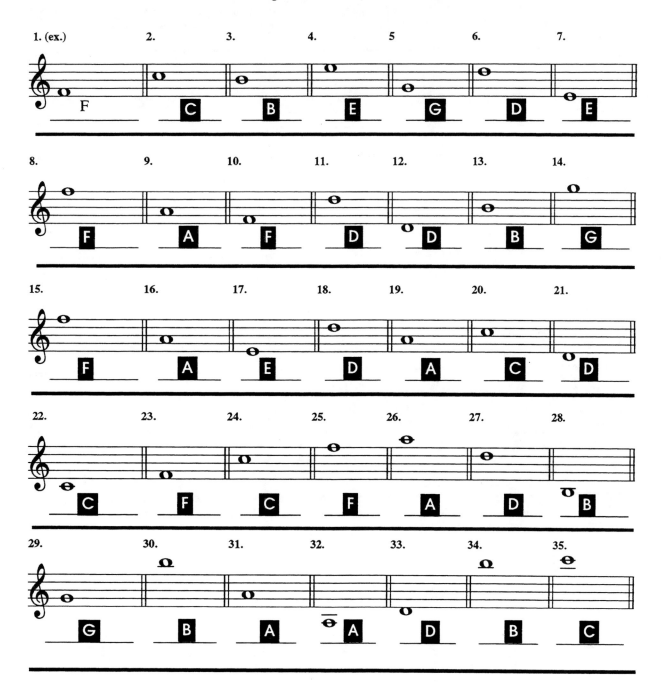

Chapter 2 (p. 21)–Assignment 4b: Octaves in the treble staff

Write notes an octave above the given notes:

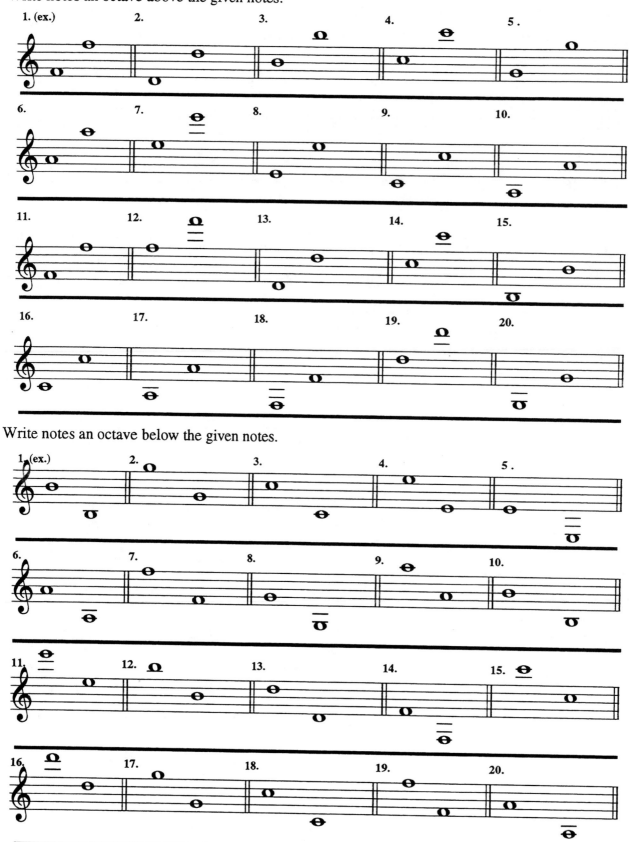

Write notes an octave below the given notes.

Chapter 2 (p. 22)–Assignment 5a:
Names of notes in the bass staff

Write the names of each of the following notes in the blanks below:

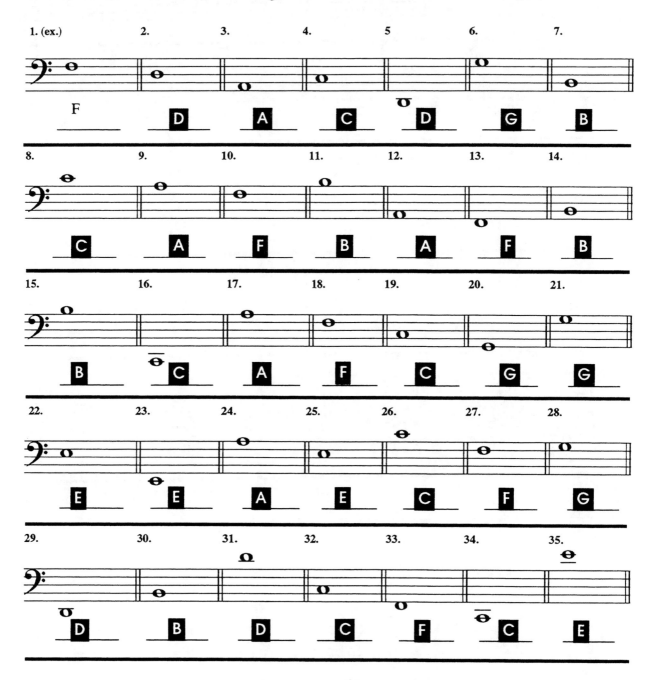

Chapter 2 (p. 22)–Assignment 5b: Octaves in the bass staff

Write notes an octave above each of the given notes:

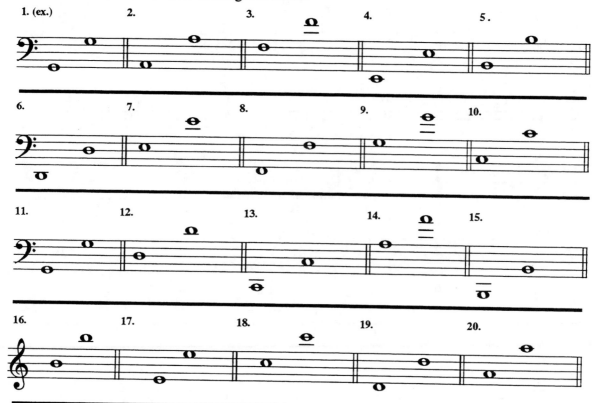

Write notes an octave below and in the bass staff from each of the treble staff notes:

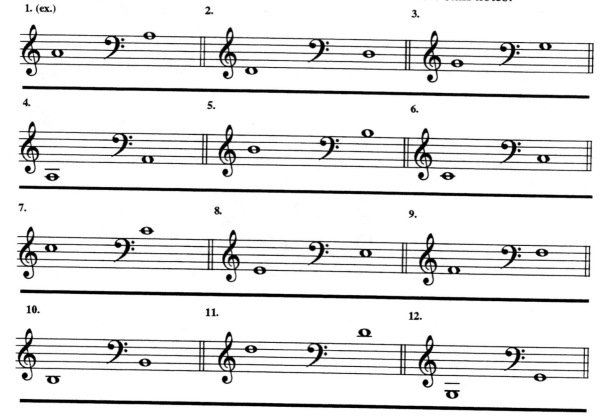

Chapter 2 (p. 23)–Assignment 6a:
Names of notes on the grand staff

Write the name of each note in the blanks below:

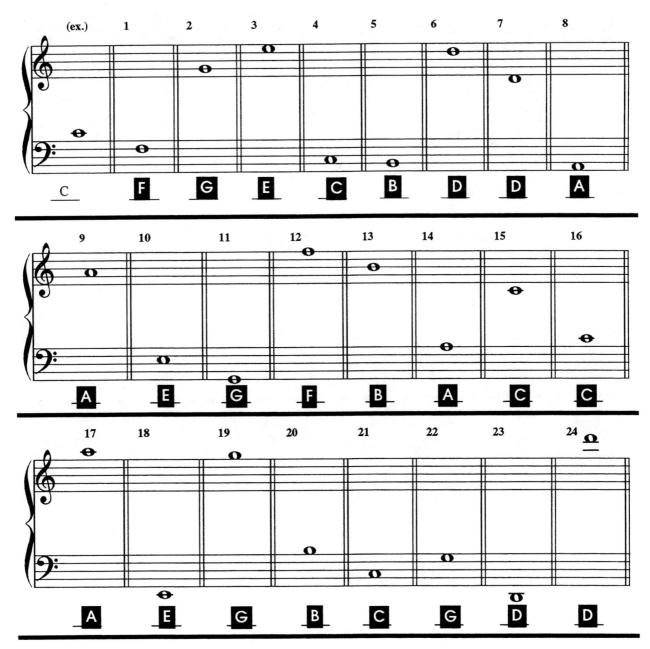

Chapter 2 (p. 23)–Assignment 6b: Octaves on the grand staff

Write notes in other octaves for each of the given notes on the grand staff. You should write at least three notes for each problem. (See example.)

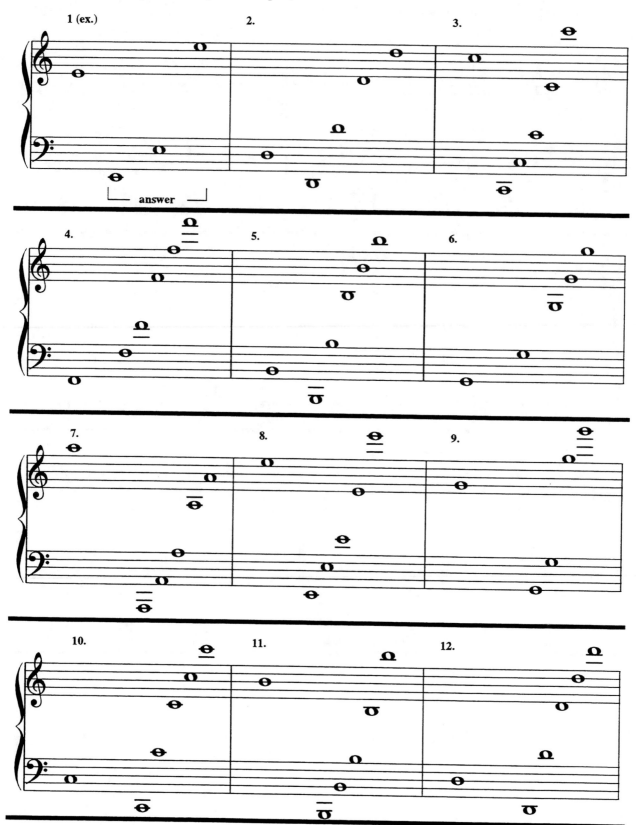

Chapter 2 (p. 27)–Assignment 7:
Drawing musical symbols

Draw five each of the following symbols. Compare your work with the symbols in figures 2.24 through 2.31.

Treble clefs:

Bass clefs:

Quarter notes
with stems up:

Quarter notes
with stems down:

Eighth notes
with flags (stems up):

Eighth notes
with flags (stems down):

Eighth notes
with beams (stems up):

Eighth notes
with beams (stems down):

Half notes
with stems up:

Half notes
with stems down:

Whole notes:

Quarter rests:

Half rests:

Eighth rests:

Whole rests:

Dotted quarter rests:

Dotted eighth rests:

Chapter 3 (p. 35)–Assignment 8:
Counting in simple meter

Draw the bar lines in the proper places in the following rhythms as indicated by the meter signature. Count the number of measures and write this number on the blank at the right.

Chapter 3 (p. 40)–Assignment 9a:
Equivalent notation in simple meters

Rewrite the following rhythms in the time signatures indicated so that they will sound exactly the same as the original rhythms. (See example.)

Chapter 3 (p. 40)–Assignment 9b: Writing rhythms in simple meters

Write rhythms in each of the following meters. Check each measure to see if it has exactly the proper number of beats. Write the counting beneath each of the rhythms.

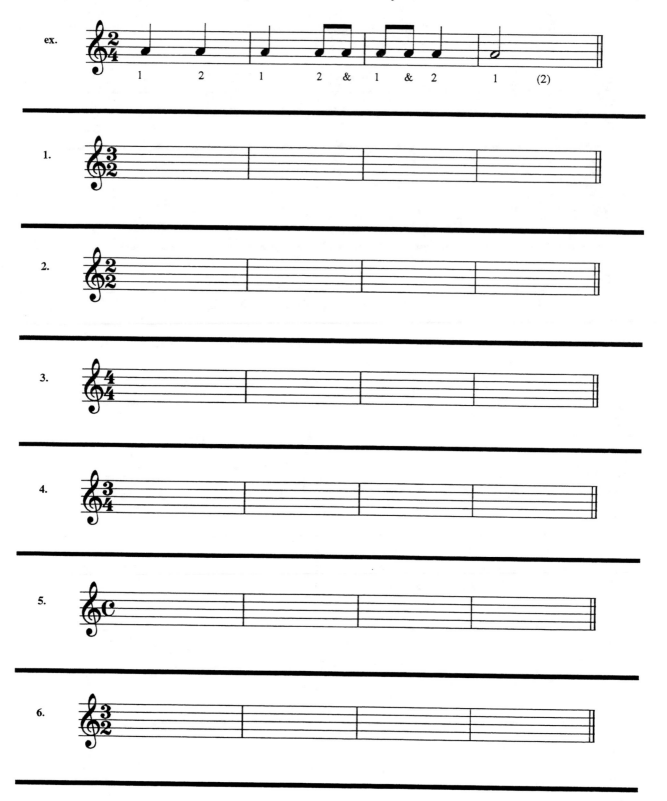

Chapter 3 (p. 44)–Assignment 10:
Identifying simple meter signatures

Write the correct meter signature for each of the following rhythms. There may be more than one correct answer. If so, write both meter signatures. (See example.)

Music First!

Chapter 4 (p. 54)–Assignment 11a:
Counting compound meters

Draw bar lines in the correct places in the following rhythmic patterns. Count the number of measures and place the number in the blank to the right. (See example.)

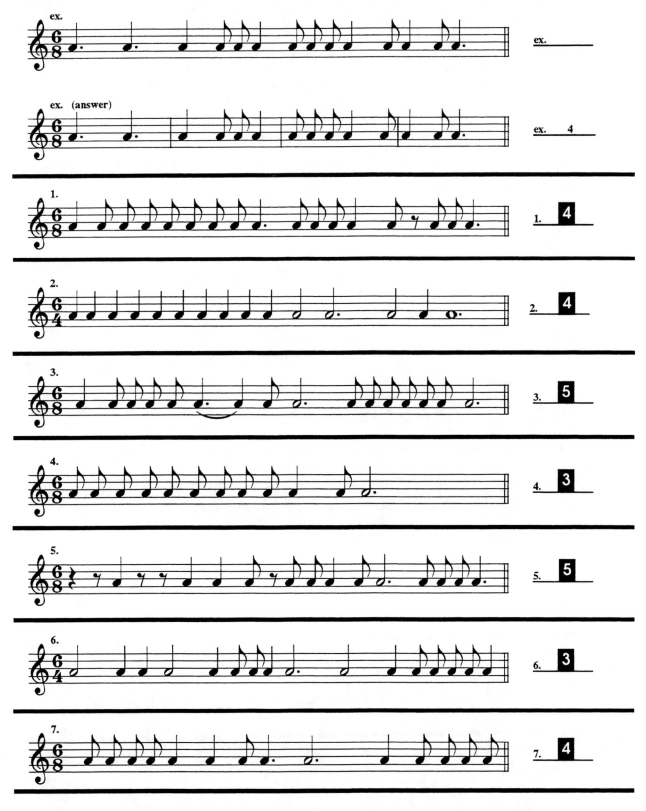

ex. _____

ex.   4

1.   **4**

2.   **4**

3.   **5**

4.   **3**

5.   **5**

6.   **3**

7.   **4**

Chapter 4 (p. 54)–Assignment 11b: Supply the missing note

Each measure in the following rhythmic patterns is missing one note. Complete each measure by adding a single note. (See example.)

Chapter 4 (p. 56)–Assignment 12a:
Meter classification of songs

Look at each of the following songs in the songbook. Write the meter signature, the meter classification (duple-simple, triple-compound, etc.), the note value receiving one beat, and the normal division of the beat. (See example.)

Song	Meter Signature	Meter Classification	Beat	Division
	$\frac{6}{8}$	Duple - compound	(dotted quarter)	(three eighth notes)
"Aura Lee" (p. 188)	$\frac{4}{4}$	Quadruple - Simple	(quarter)	(two eighth notes)
"Barbara Allen" (p. 188)	$\frac{3}{4}$	Triple - Simple	(quarter)	(two eighth notes)
"Billy Boy" (p. 190)	$\frac{2}{4}$	Duple - Simple	(quarter)	(two eighth notes)
"Caisson Song "(p. 191)	$\frac{2}{2}$	Duple - Simple	(half)	(two quarter notes)
"Down in the Valley" (p. 197)	$\frac{9}{8}$	Triple - Compound	(dotted quarter)	(three eighth notes)
Six Rounds in Major Keys - number 6 (p. 224)	$\frac{6}{4}$	Duple - Compound	(dotted half)	(three quarter notes)
Three Rounds in Minor Keys - number 3 (p. 228)	$\frac{4}{4}$ C	Quadruple - Simple	(quarter)	(two eighth notes)
"When the Saints Go Marching In" (p. 232)	$\frac{2}{2}$ ¢	Duple - Simple	(half)	(two quarter notes)

Chapter 4 (p. 56)–Assignment 12b: Counting compound meters

Draw bar lines in the correct places in the following rhythmic patterns. Count the number of measures and place the number in the blank to the right. (See example.)

ex.

ex.   4

1.   **3**

2.   **4**

3.   **3**

4.   **3**

5.   **2**

6.   **4**

7.   **3**

Chapter 4 (p. 57)–Assignment 13a:
Supply the missing note

Each measure in the following rhythmic patterns is missing one note. Complete each measure by adding a single note. (See example.)

Chapter 4 (p. 57)–Assignment 13b: Meter classification

For each of the following meter signatures list the meter classification (duple-compound, triple-simple, etc.), the note value that receives one beat, and the normal division of the beat. (See example.)

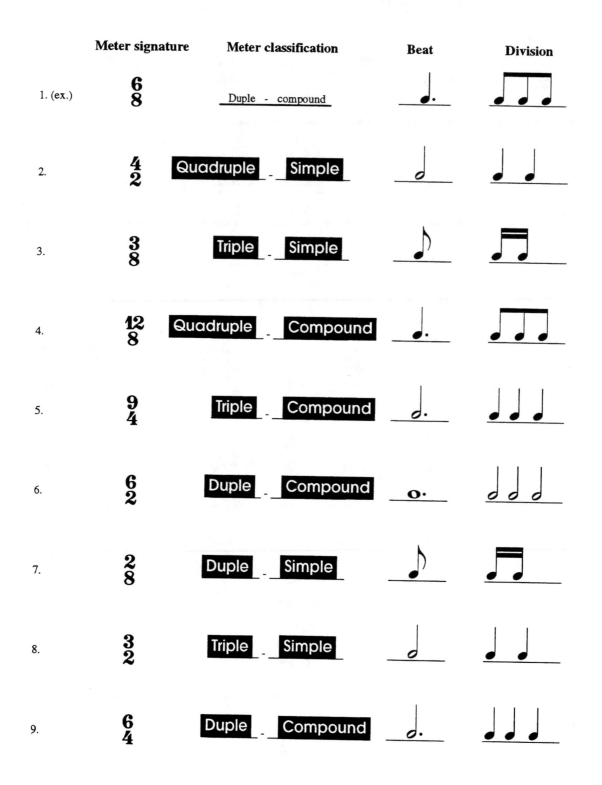

	Meter signature	Meter classification	Beat	Division
1. (ex.)	6/8	Duple - compound		
2.	4/2	Quadruple - Simple		
3.	3/8	Triple - Simple		
4.	12/8	Quadruple - Compound		
5.	9/4	Triple - Compound		
6.	6/2	Duple - Compound		
7.	2/8	Duple - Simple		
8.	3/2	Triple - Simple		
9.	6/4	Duple - Compound		

Chapter 5 (p. 69)–Assignment 14:
Enharmonic notation

Write each of the indicated black keys, first as a sharp and then as a flat. (See example.)

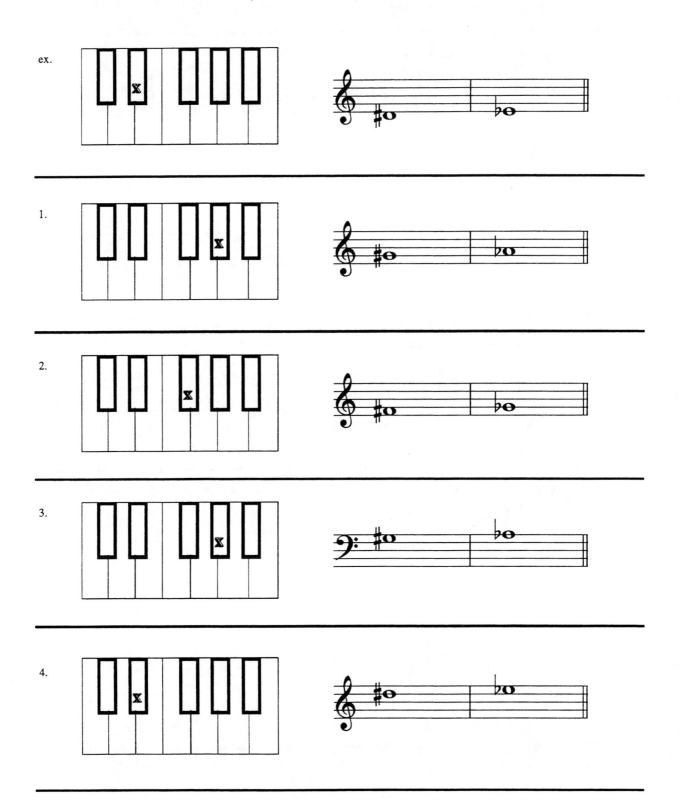

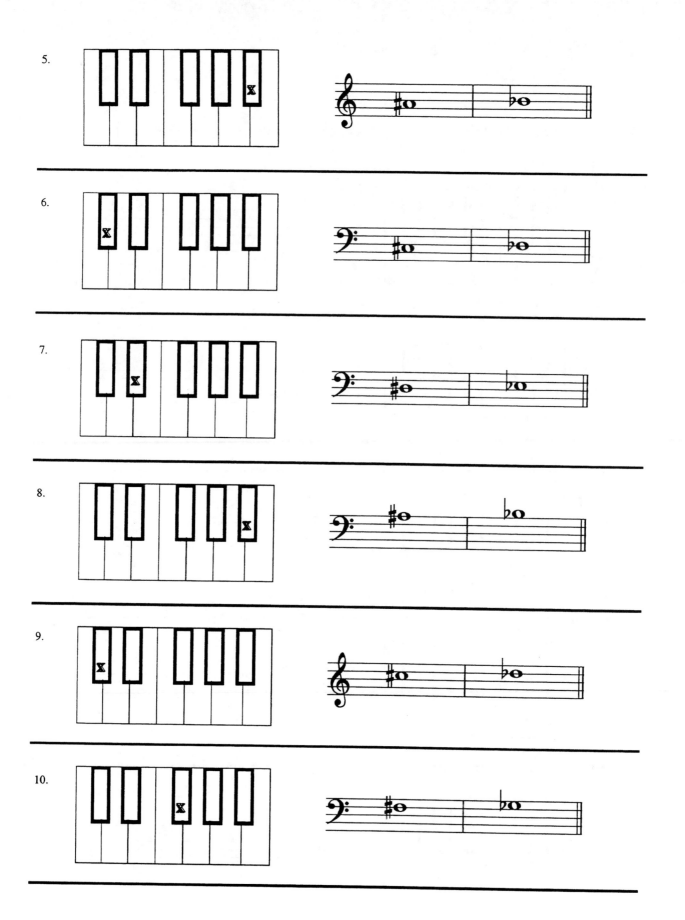

Chapter 5 (p. 71)–Assignment 15a:
Writing whole and half steps above

Write whole or half steps as requested above each of the following notes. There may be more than one correct answer.

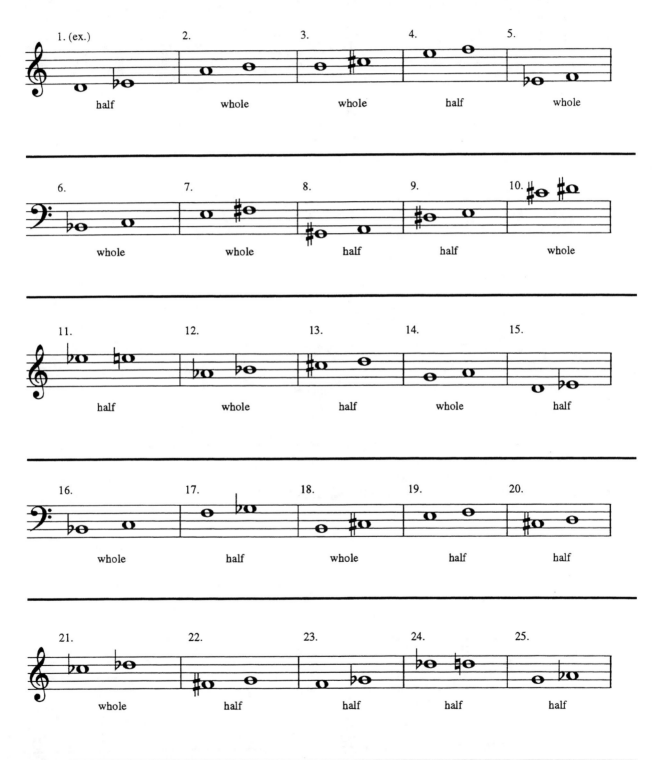

Chapter 5 (p. 71)–Assignment 15b: Writing whole and half steps below

Write whole or half steps as requested below each of the following notes. There may be more than one correct answer.

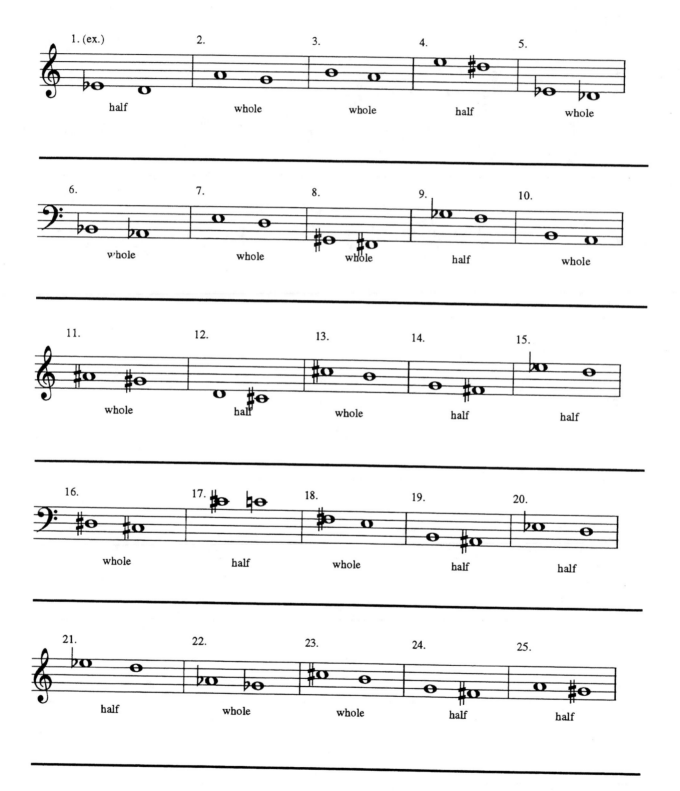

Chapter 6 (p. 79)–Assignment 16a:
Determining the major key and scale

Determine the key for each of the following songs by first forming the scale as described on page 78.

1. **"Aura Lee":** 188

   Pitch collection:

   Scale:

   Key: **F**

2. **"All Creatures of Our God and King":** 185

   Pitch collection:

   Scale:

   Key: **D**

3. **"I Never Will Marry":** 201

   Pitch collection:

   Scale:

   Key: **F**

4. **Pictures at an Exhibition, no. 10 -- "The Great Gate of Kiev":** 217

   Pitch collection:

   Scale:

   Key: **E-flat**

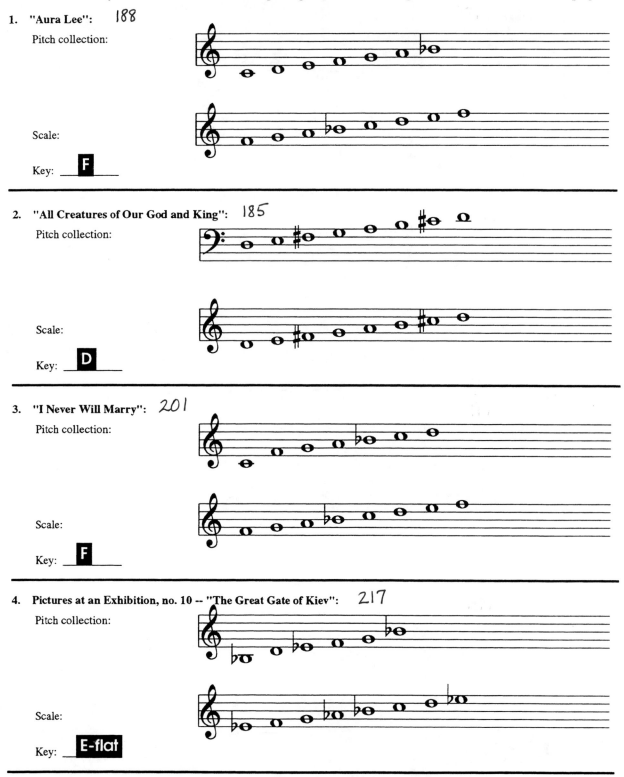

Chapter 6 (p. 79)–Assignment 16b: Determining the major key and scale

Determine the key for each of the following songs by first forming the scale as described on page 78.

1. **"Barbara Allen":** 188
   Pitch collection:

   Scale:

   Key: **D**

2. **"Billy Boy":** 190
   Pitch collection:

   Scale:

   Key: **D**

3. **"Caisson Song":** 191
   Pitch collection:

   Scale:

   Key: **C**

4. *Cielito Lindo:* 194
   Pitch collection:

   Scale:

   Key: **A**

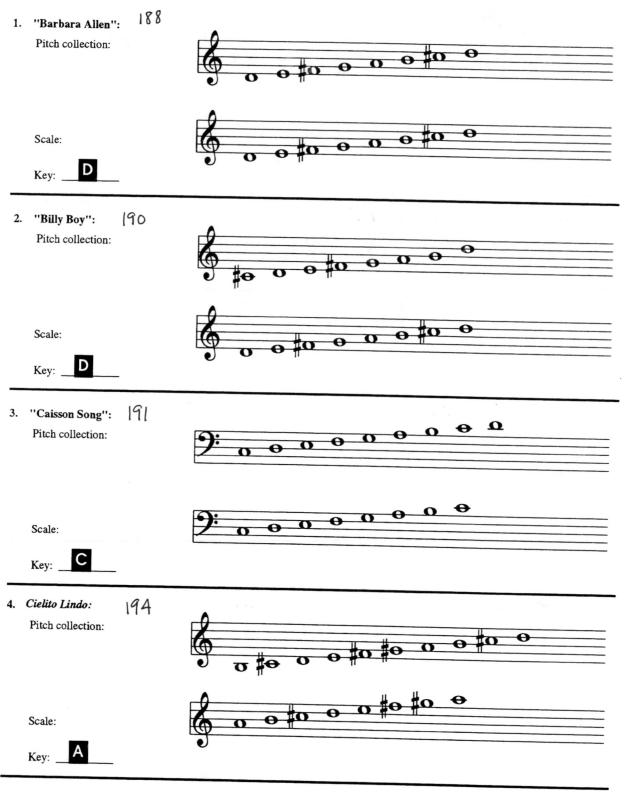

Chapter 6 (p. 82)–Assignment 17a:
Major scales on the keyboard

1. Mark the tones of a major scale on the keyboard, starting on the key marked with an "X."

2. Write the scale on the staff provided, using accidentals. (Remember that there must be only one of each letter name in the scale.)

3. Write the proper key signature for the scale on the second staff. (See example.)

(For reference, the key signatures of 7 sharps and 7 flats are shown in both treble and bass staves below.)

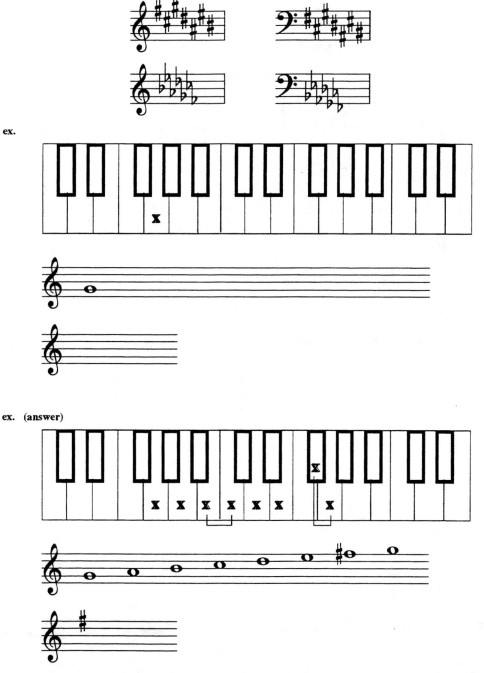

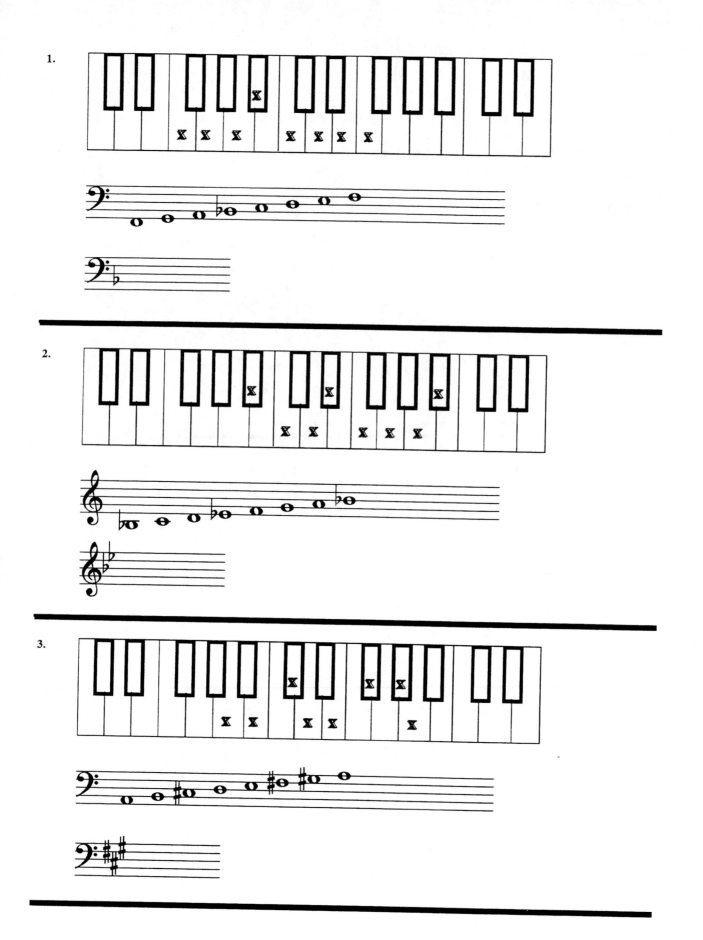

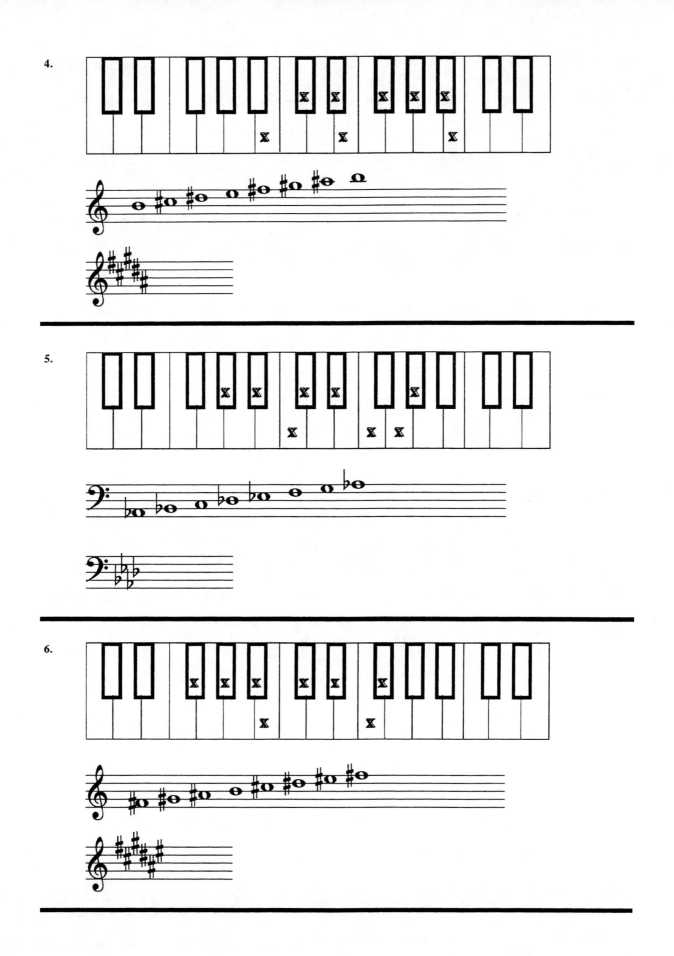

Chapter 6 (p. 82)–Assignment 17b: Major scales on the keyboard

Write the proper key signature for each of the following major scales and then write the scale. (See example.)

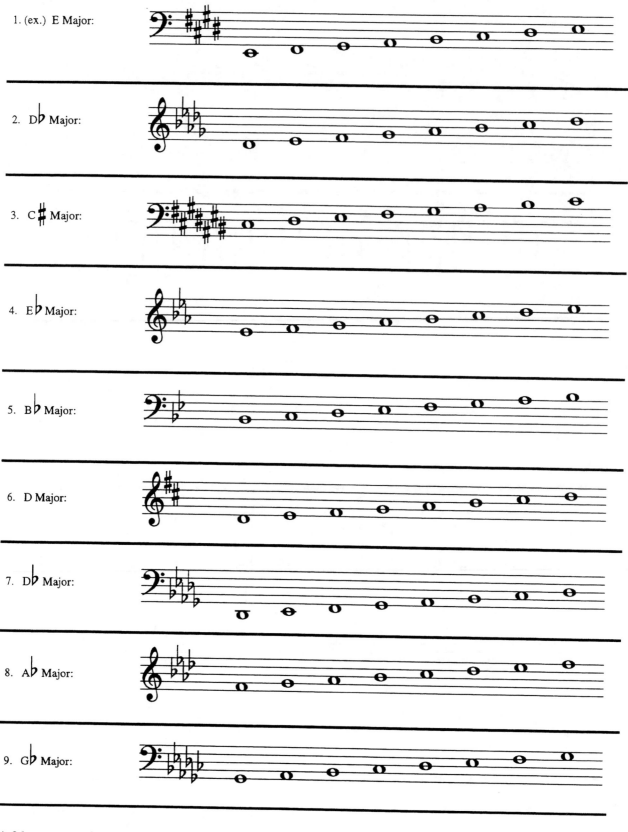

1. (ex.) E Major:

2. D♭ Major:

3. C♯ Major:

4. E♭ Major:

5. B♭ Major:

6. D Major:

7. D♭ Major:

8. A♭ Major:

9. G♭ Major:

Chapter 6 (p. 83)–Assignment 18a:
Major key signatures–tonic and dominant

Name the major key for each of the following key signatures and write the tonic and dominant on the staff. (See example.)

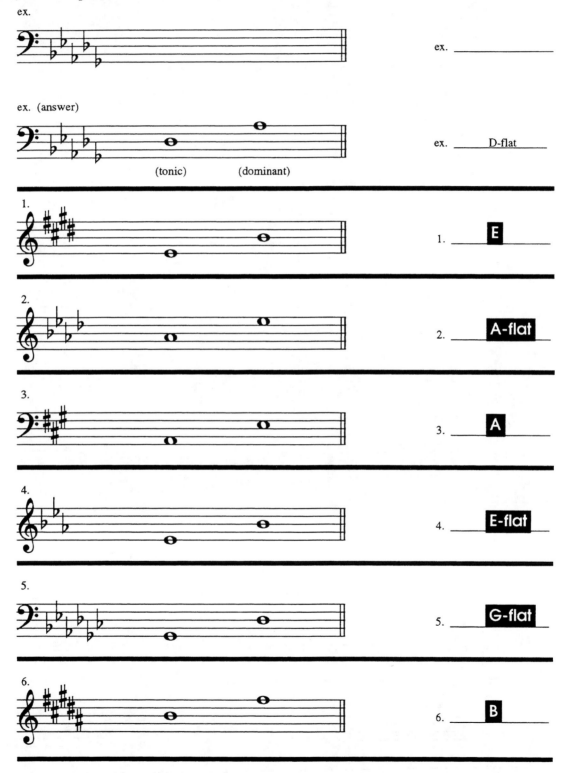

ex. _____

ex. (answer)

(tonic)   (dominant)

ex. _____ D-flat _____

1. _____ **E**

2. _____ **A-flat**

3. _____ **A**

4. _____ **E-flat**

5. _____ **G-flat**

6. _____ **B**

Chapter 6 (p. 83)–Assignment 18b: Writing key signatures for major keys

Write the key signature for each of the following major scales. (See example.)

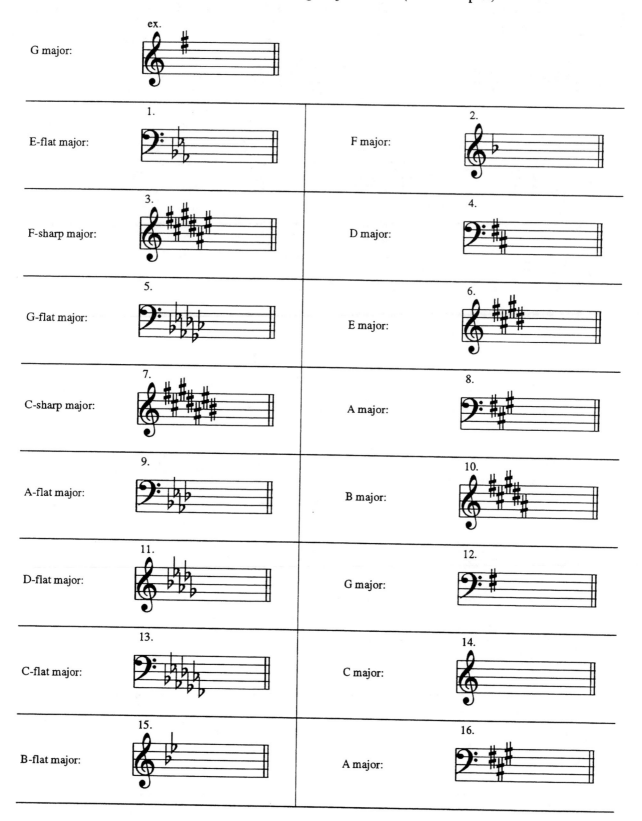

Chapter 7 (p. 93)–Assignment 19a: Interval Identification

Write the specific name of each interval (M3, P4, etc.) on the blank below.

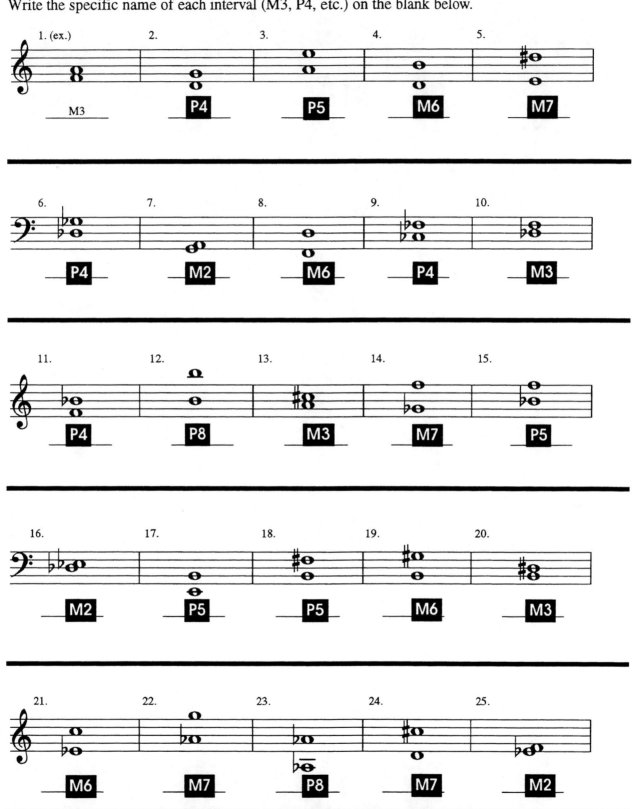

Chapter 7 (p. 93)–Assignment 19b: Interval Identification

Name each interval (M3, P4, etc.) in the following melody on the blanks below.

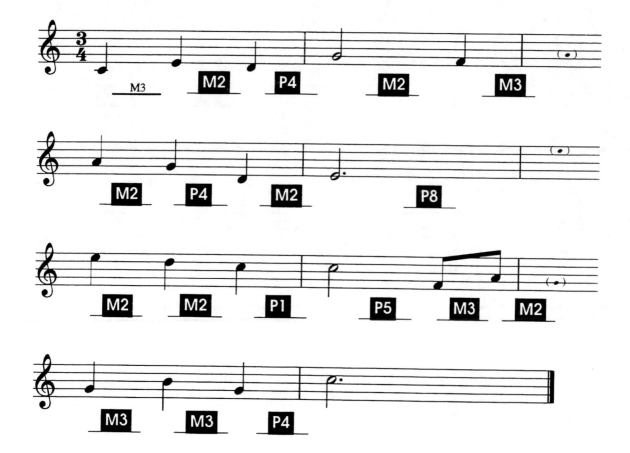

Chapter 7 (p. 97)–Assignment 20a:
Inversion of intervals

Write the inversion of each of the given intervals and name both the interval and its inversion.

1. (ex.)   2.   3.

P5   P4   M3   m6   m7   M2

4.   5.   6.

P8   P1   d5   A4   M2   m7

7.   8.   9.

d5   A4   m2   M7   P4   P5

10.   11.   12.

m3   M6   m6   M3   P5   P4

13.   14.   15.

M7   m2   m2   M7   M6   m3

Chapter 7 (p. 97)–Assignment 20b: Intervals in a melody

Write the name of each interval in "Scarborough Fair" on the blanks below the melody.

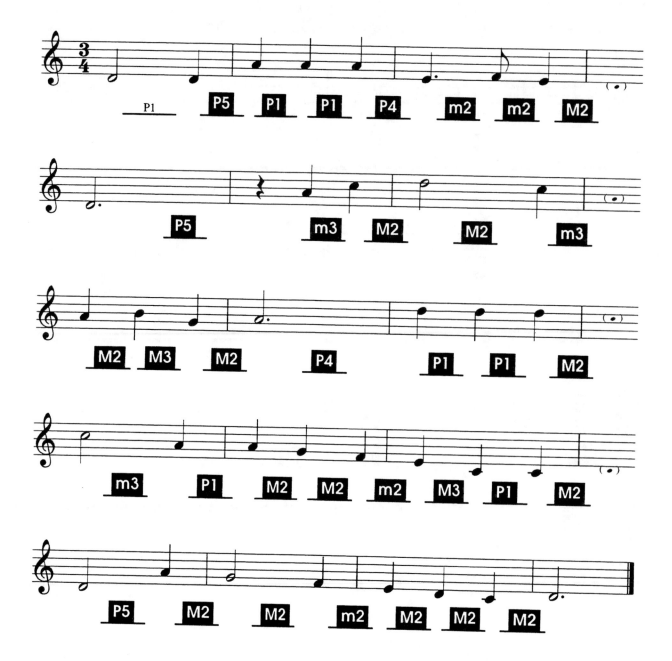

Chapter 7 (p. 97)–Assignment 21a:
Writing intervals above and below

Write the requested interval both above and below the given notes. (See example.)

Chapter 7 (p. 97)–Assignment 21b: Writing intervals above and below

Same instructions as 21a.

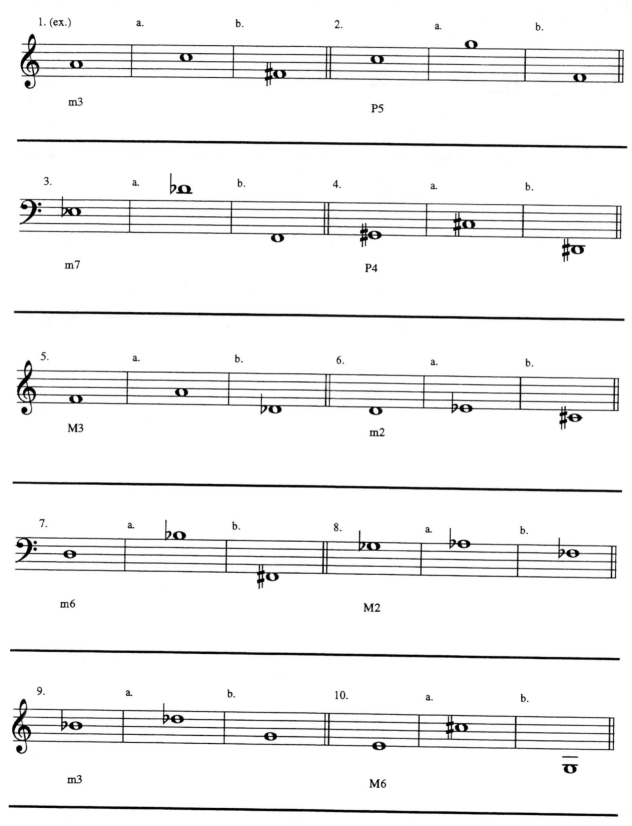

Chapter 8 (p. 106)–Assignment 22: Determining minor keys and scales

Determine the minor scale in each of the following songs by first making a pitch collection as described on page 78. Fill in the tonic and the probable form of the scale in the blanks on the right. (In some cases you will not be able to tell for sure due to missing scale degrees.)

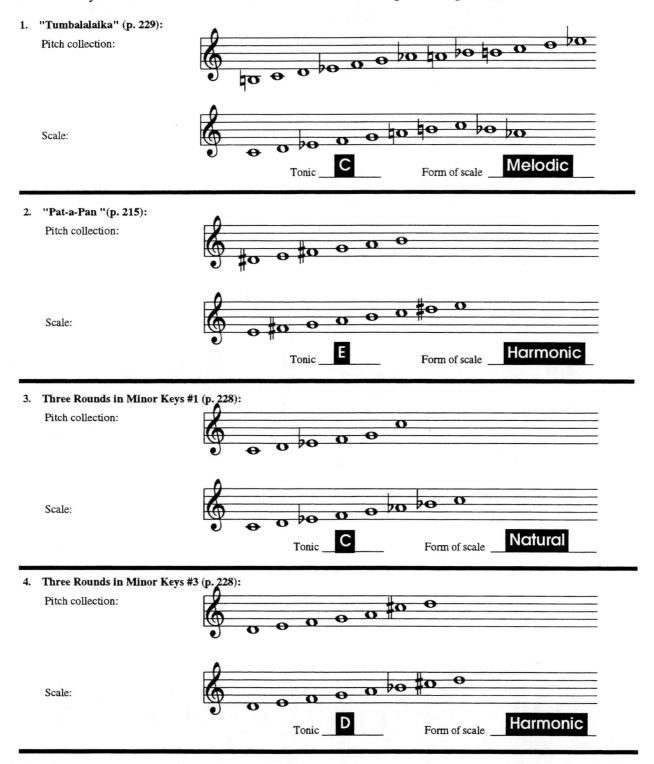

Chapter 8 (p. 109)–Assignment 23a:
Minor scales on the keyboard

1. Mark the tones of the given form of minor scale on the keyboard starting on the key marked with an "X."

2. Write the scale on the staff provided, using accidentals. (Remember that there must be only one of each letter name in the scale.)

3. Write the proper key signature for the scale on the second staff. (See example for assignment 17a.)

(For reference, the key signatures of 7 sharps and 7 flats are shown in both treble and bass staves below.)

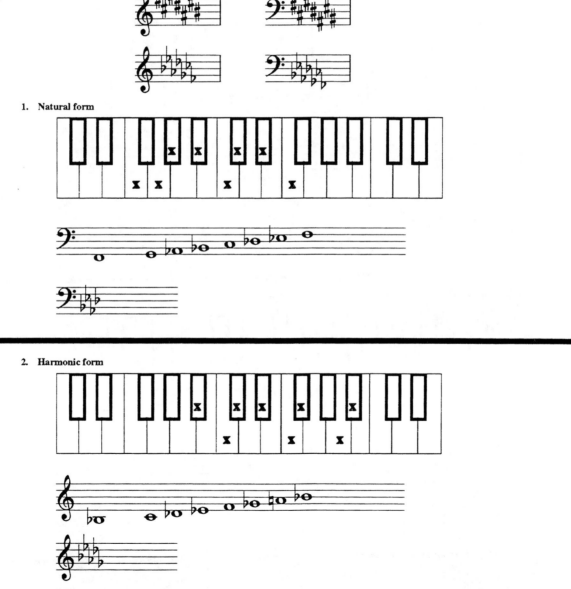

3. Melodic (ascending)

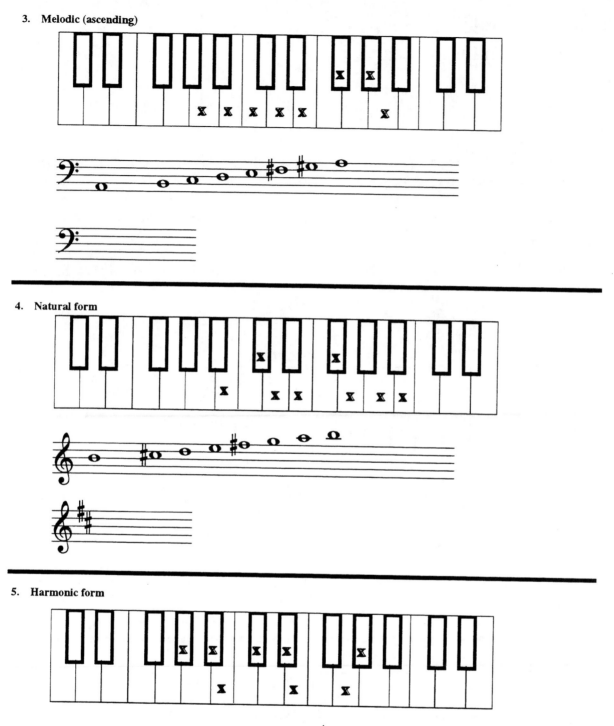

4. Natural form

5. Harmonic form

Chapter 8 (p. 109)–Assignment 23b:
Minor scales on the keyboard

Write the proper key signature for each of the following minor scales and then write the scale in the form indicated. (See example.)

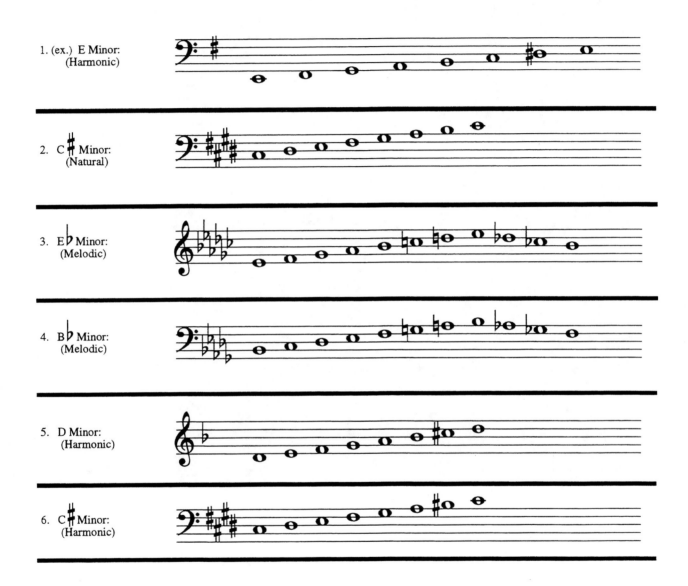

1. (ex.) E Minor: (Harmonic)

2. C♯ Minor: (Natural)

3. E♭ Minor: (Melodic)

4. B♭ Minor: (Melodic)

5. D Minor: (Harmonic)

6. C♯ Minor: (Harmonic)

Chapter 8 (p. 112)–Assignment 24a:
Transposition

Transpose the following round by Haydn (Three Rounds in Minor Keys, #2), from F-sharp minor to G minor.

Transpose the following round by Webbe (Six Rounds in Major Keys, #4), from F major to A major.

Chapter 8 (p. 112)–Assignment 24b: Naming major and minor keys

Write the major and the minor keys for each of the following key signatures. (See example.)

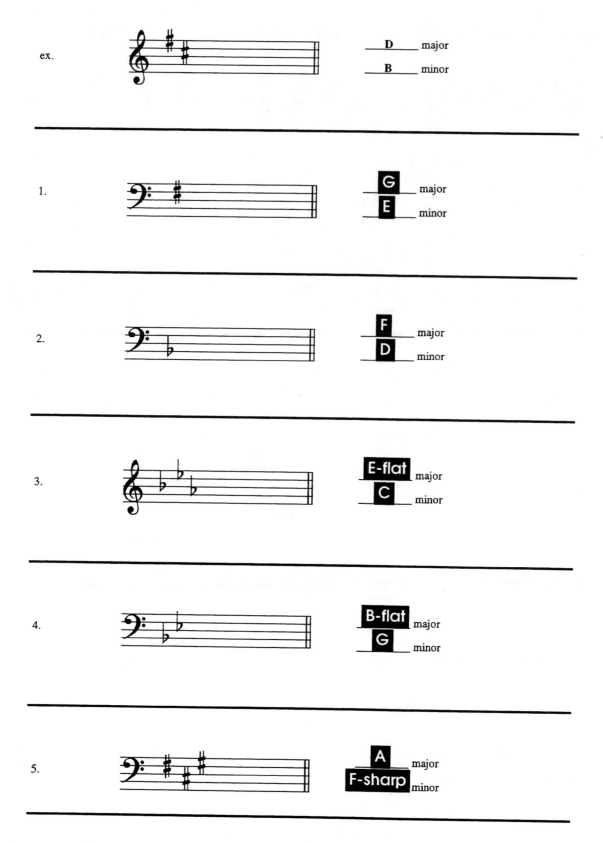

ex.   **D** major
              B minor

1.   **G** major
              E minor

2.   **F** major
              D minor

3.   **E-flat** major
              C minor

4.   **B-flat** major
              G minor

5.   **A** major
              F-sharp minor

Chapter 9 (p. 119)–Assignment 25a:
Popular music chord symbols

Write the popular music chord symbols for each of the following chords in the box above:

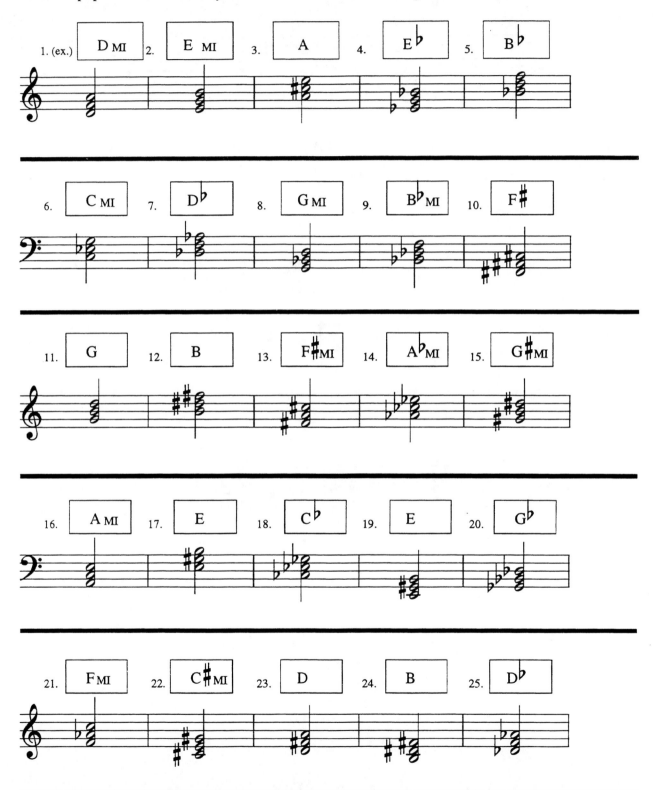

Chapter 9 (p. 119)–Assignment 25b: Writing major and minor triads

Write the major and minor triads requested below each popular music chord symbol.

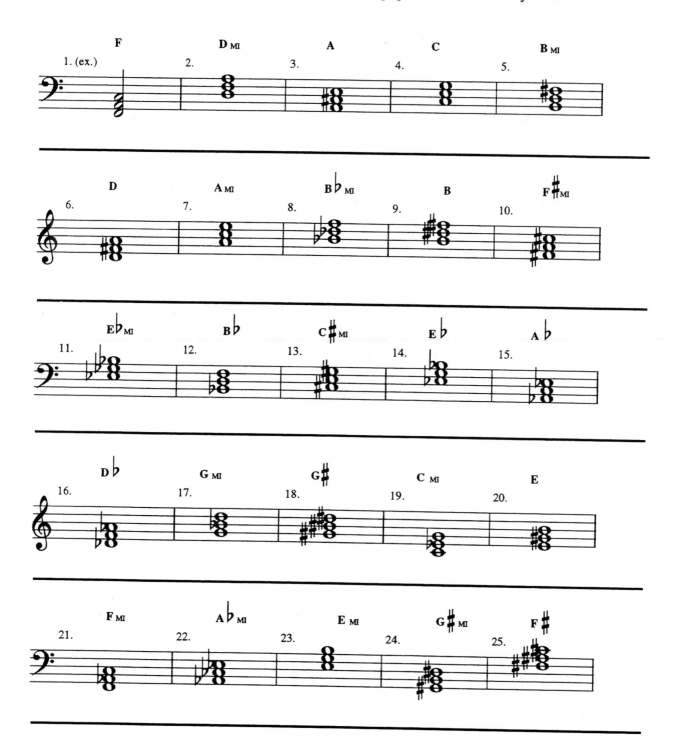

Chapter 9 (p. 120)–Assignment 26a:
Popular music chord symbols

Write the popular music chord symbols for each of the following chords in the box above:

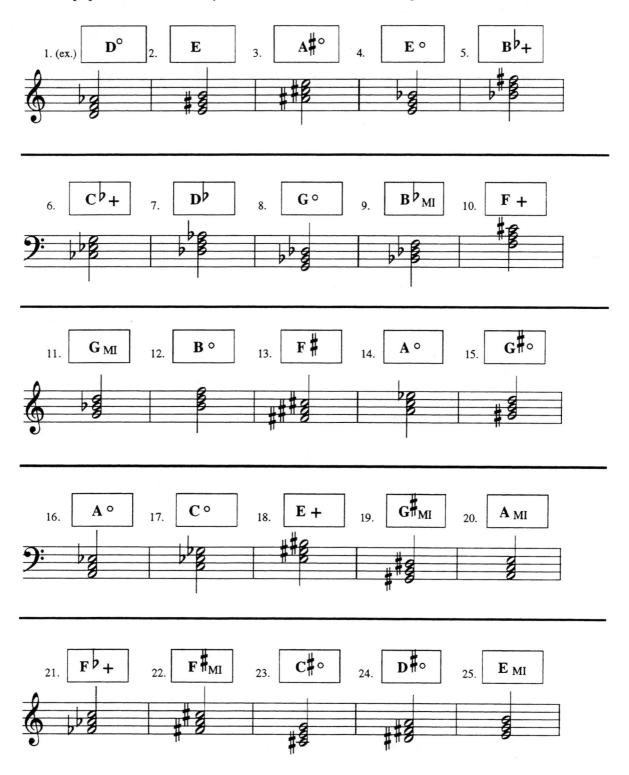

Chapter 9 (p. 120)–Assignment 26b: Writing triads

Write the major, minor, augmented, or diminished triads requested below each popular music chord symbol.

Chapter 9 (p. 124)–Assignment 27a:
Popular music chord symbols

Write the chords indicated by the popular music chord symbols on the bass staff below the melody "Aura Lee." Use whole notes for each chord.

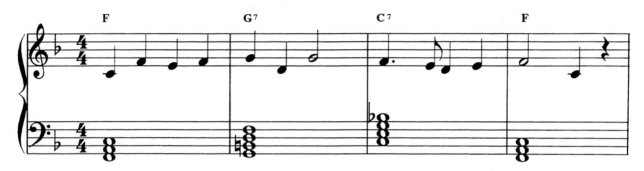

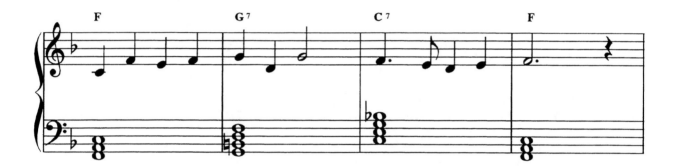

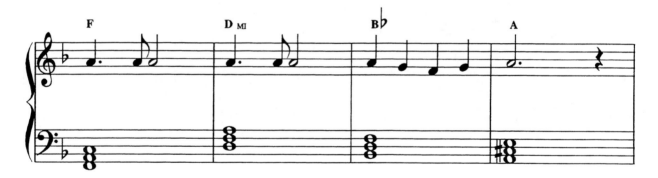

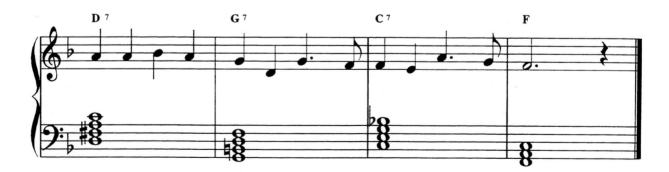

Chapter 9 (p. 124)–Assignment 27b: Popular music chord symbols

Write the chords indicated by the popular music chord symbols on the bass staff below the melody "God of Our Fathers." Use proper note values for each chord as indicated. (Melody and chord note values may differ. Be sure the chords in each measure add up to four beats.)

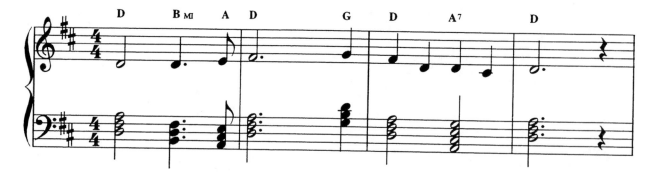

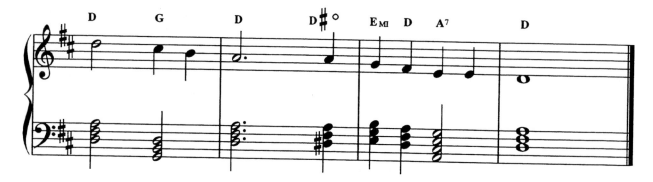

Chapter 9 (p. 124)–Assignment 28a:
Finding chords in music literature

Examine the sections of the following excerpts from music literature contained in the numbered boxes. Each box contains a single chord. Write the chord in simple position on the staff in the proper box below and provide a popular music chord symbol for the chord. Be sure to look at the clefs and key signatures. (See example.)

Schubert: Sonata for Piano, op. 122 (trio)

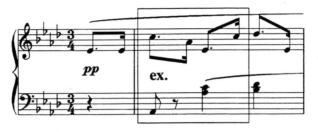

Mendelssohn: Songs Without Words, op. 30, no. 3

Haydn: Sonata no. 8 in A Major, Hob. XVI/5 (second movement)

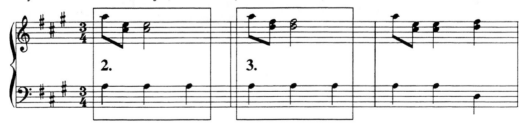

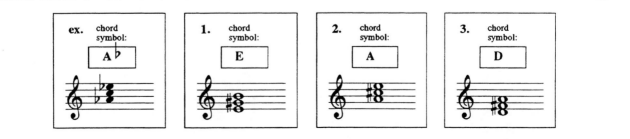

von Weber: *Theme from Variations über ein Original Thema*, op. 2

4.   **5.**

Schubert: Sonatina for Violin and Piano, op. 137, no. 3

6.   **7.**

| 4. chord symbol: G⁷ | 5. chord symbol: C | 6. chord symbol: E♭ | 7. chord symbol: B♭⁷ |

Beethoven: Sonata, op. 79, third movement

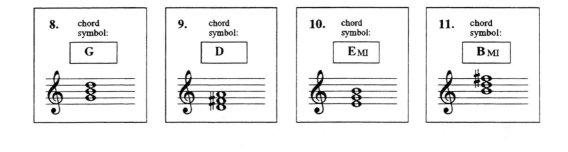

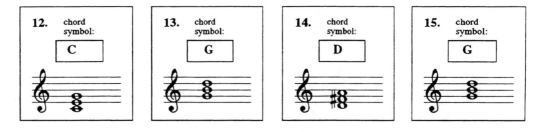

Schubert: *Die Schöne Müllerin*, op. 25, no. 2

Ich __ hört' ein Bäch - lein   rau - schen wohl __

16.

Chopin: Mazurka 43 in G Minor, op. 67, no. 2

17.

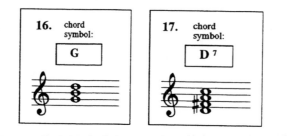

16. chord symbol:

G

17. chord symbol:

D 7

Chapter 9 (p.124)–Assignment 28b:
Finding chords in music literature

Examine the sections of the following excerpts from music literature contained in the numbered boxes. Each box contains a single chord. Write the chord in simple position on the staff in the proper box below and provide a popular music chord symbol for the chord. Be sure to look at the clefs and key signatures.

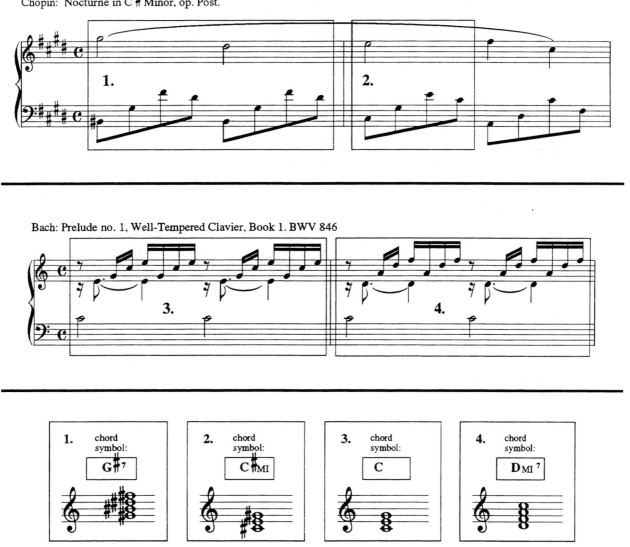

Chopin: Nocturne in C♯ Minor, op. Post.

Bach: Prelude no. 1, Well-Tempered Clavier, Book 1. BWV 846

Schumann: Ich grolle nicht, *Dichterliebe,* no. 7

Mendelssohn: Songs Without Words, op. 30, no. 6

Brahms: *Wiegenlied,* op. 49, no. 4

9.

Gu - ten A - bend, Gut' Nacht, mit

Mozart: Theme with Variations, K. 284

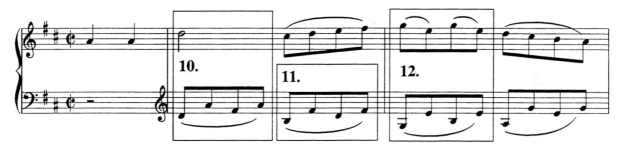

10.

11.

12.

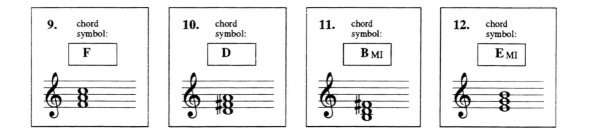

Chopin: Mazurka 5 in B♭ Major, op. 7, no. 1

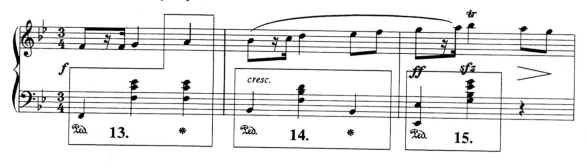

Schubert: *Der König in Thule,* D. 367

Es   war   ein   Kön - ig   in   Thu -   le,

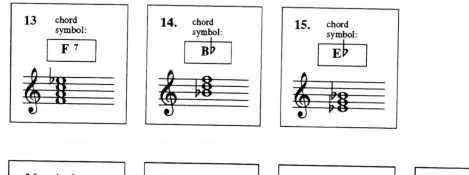

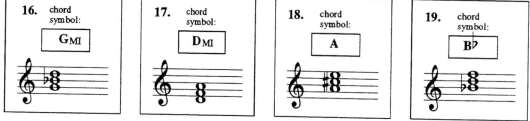

Chapter 10 (p. 130)–Assignment 29a:
Chord analysis in songs

Look at the chords for each of the following songs and write each of the chords called for by popular music chord symbols, using the tones of the scale provided as the root. If both a triad and a seventh chord occur on a single scale degree, write the seventh chord. Write the key followed by a colon, followed by the correct roman numeral under each of the chords. Remember that upper case roman numerals are used for major triads and lower case roman numerals indicate minor triads. (See the example.)

ex.   **"Skip to My Lou" - F major (p. 226):**

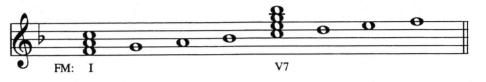

1.   **"Love Somebody "- C major (p. 208):**

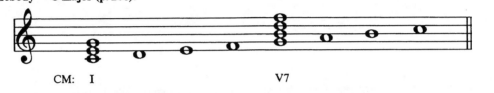

2.   **"I've Got To Know "- E major (p. 203):**

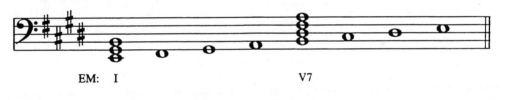

3.   **"Lavender's Blue "- D major (p. 205):**

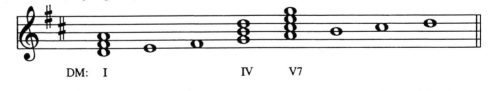

4.   **"Battle Hymn of the Republic" - B-flat major (p. 189):**

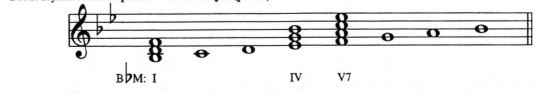

5. *Dona Nobis Pacem* - F major (p. 196)

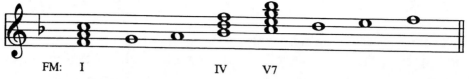

FM: I   IV   V7

6. "Barbara Allen"- D major (p. 188)

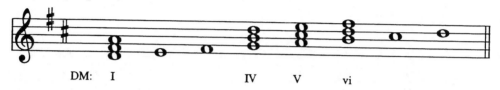

DM: I   IV   V   vi

7. "Sweet Betsy from Pike"- C major (p. 226)

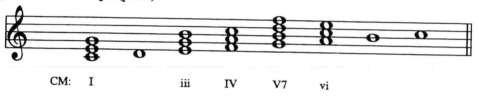

CM: I   iii   IV   V7   vi

8. "The First Noël" - C major (p.198)

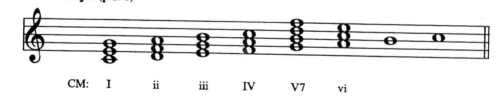

CM: I   ii   iii   IV   V7   vi

9. "Saturday Night "- D major (p. 221)

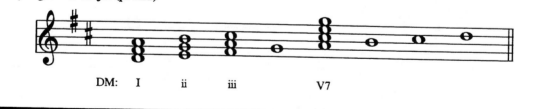

DM: I   ii   iii   V7

10. "We Shall Overcome"- C major (p. 232)

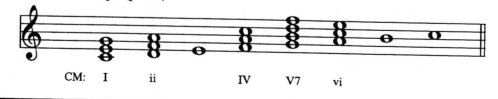

CM: I   ii   IV   V7   vi

Chapter 10 (p. 130)–Assignment 29b:
Primary triads in major keys

Write the primary triads (I,IV,V) in each of the following major keys. Remember to write the proper key signature in each case. Label each chord with the appropriate roman numeral. (See example.)

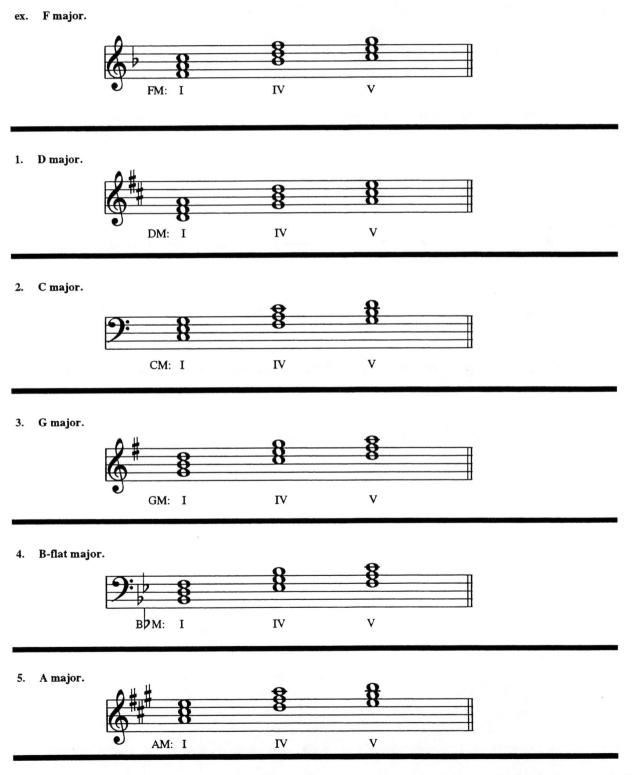

ex.   **F major.**

FM: I   IV   V

1.   **D major.**

DM: I   IV   V

2.   **C major.**

CM: I   IV   V

3.   **G major.**

GM: I   IV   V

4.   **B-flat major.**

B♭M: I   IV   V

5.   **A major.**

AM: I   IV   V

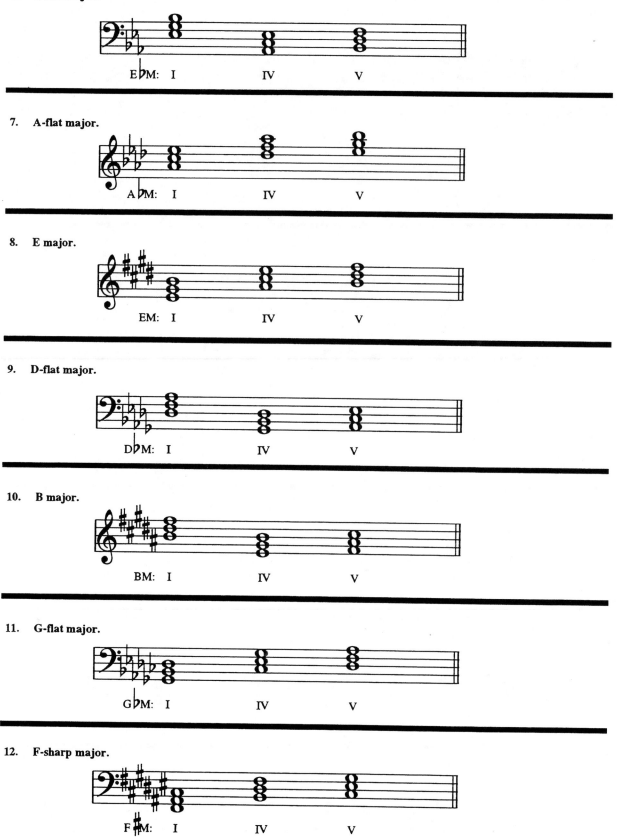

Chapter 10 (p. 135)–Assignment 30a:
Primary triads in minor

Write the primary triads (i,iv,V) in each of the following minor keys. Using the harmonic minor in each case, and remember to write the proper key signature. Label each chord with the appropriate roman numeral. (See example.)

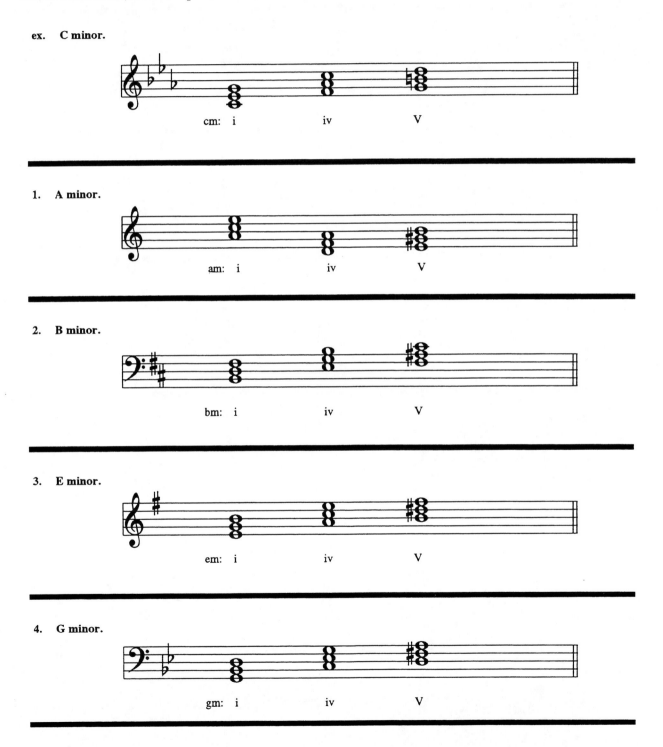

ex. C minor.

cm: i   iv   V

1. A minor.

am: i   iv   V

2. B minor.

bm: i   iv   V

3. E minor.

em: i   iv   V

4. G minor.

gm: i   iv   V

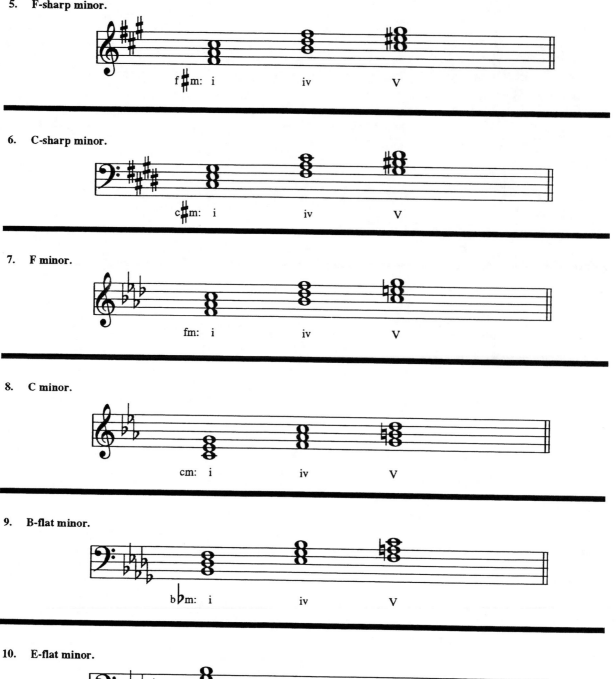

5. F-sharp minor.

f♯m: i   iv   V

6. C-sharp minor.

c♯m: i   iv   V

7. F minor.

fm: i   iv   V

8. C minor.

cm: i   iv   V

9. B-flat minor.

b♭m: i   iv   V

10. E-flat minor.

e♭m: i   iv   V

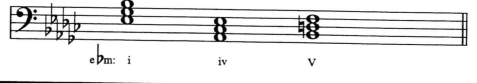

Chapter 10 (p. 135)–Assignment 30b:
Finding chords in rounds

Copy the rounds indicated on the staves below. Examine each beat in all parts and write the harmonic background on the final stave. Nonharmonic tones are circled in the songbook and should be ignored. (See chapter 11 for a discussion of these tones.) Do a roman numeral analysis of the chords implied on each beat of the measures. (See figure 10.15 for an example of the proper procedure.)

1. Six Rounds in Major Keys #4 - F major (p. 225)

2. Six Rounds in Major Keys #2 - F major (p. 224):

Harmonic Background:

FM: I   V7   I

3. "Row, Row, Row Your Boat" - C major (p. 218):

Harmonic Background:

CM: I   I   I   I

4. Three Rounds in Minor Keys #3 ("Ah Poor Bird") - D minor (p. 228):

Harmonic Background:

dm: i   V7   i

Chapter 11 (p. 144)–Assignment 31a:
Nonharmonic tones

Circle all tones that are not a part of the indicated chords in "Lavender's Blue."

See the nonharmonic tone analysis of "My Bonnie" in figure 11.3 (p. 142) for an example of the proper procedure.

Lavender's Blue

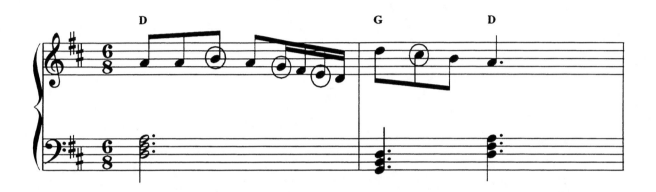

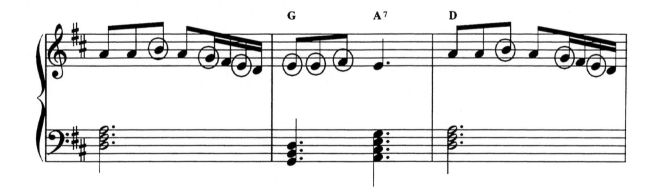

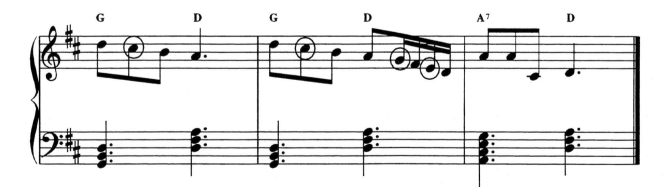

Chapter 11 (p. 144)–Assignment 31b: Nonharmonic tones

Circle all tones that are not a part of the indicated chords in "Simple Gifts."

See the nonharmonic tone analysis of "My Bonnie" in figure 11.3 (p. 142) for an example of the proper procedure.

Simple Gifts

Chapter 11 (p. 144)–Assignment 32a: Writing chords and identifying nonharmonic tones

Write each of the suggested chords in "Barbara Allen" using the correct rhythmic values to show the harmonic rhythm (see figure 11.7, p. 144). Now circle all tones that are not a part of the indicated chords.

Barbara Allen

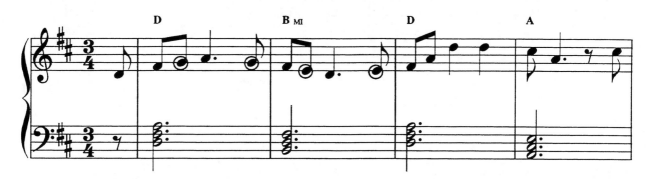

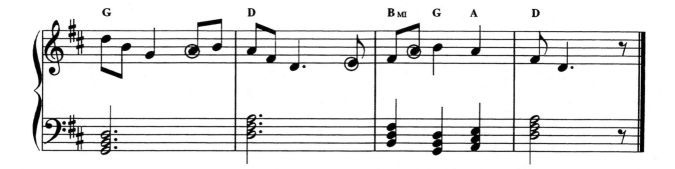

Chapter 11 (p. 144)–Assignment 32b: Writing chords and identifying nonharmonic tones

Write each of the suggested chords in "Crusader's Hymn" using the correct rhythmic values to show the harmonic rhythm (see figure 11.7, p. 144). Now circle all tones that are not a part of the indicated chords.

Crusader's Hymn

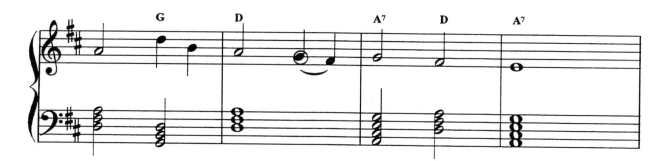

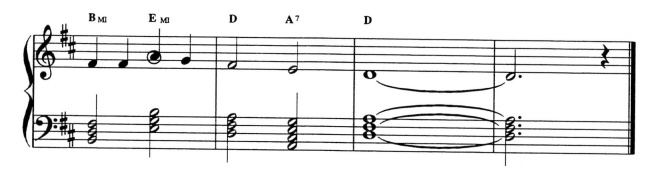

Chapter 11 (p. 151–Assignment 33a:
Cadences and phrase analysis

Divide the song *Auprès de ma Blonde* into phrases and draw the melodic contour of each phrase. Identify the cadence of each phrase by type: authentic, plagal, or half. (See figures 11.14, 11.15, 11.16 and 11.17 on pages 148-150 for the proper procedure.)

Auprès de ma Blonde

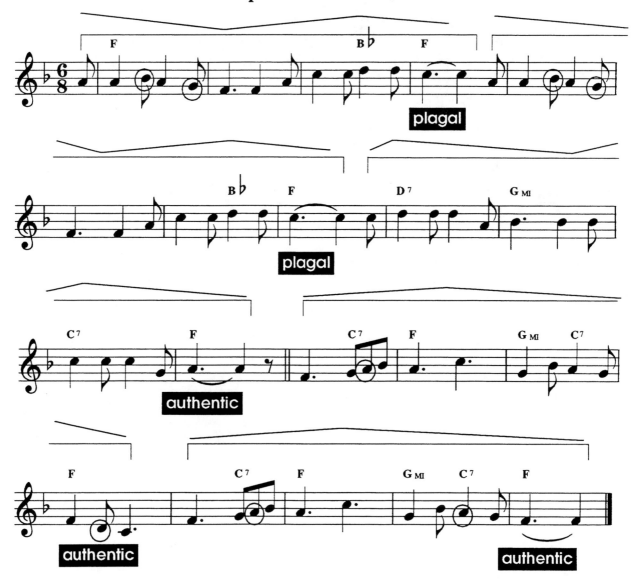

Chapter 11 (p. 151)–Assignment 33b: Cadences and phrase analysis

Divide the song "I Saw Three Ships" into phrases and draw the melodic contour of each phrase. Identify the cadence of each phrase by type: authentic, plagal, or half. (See figures 11.14, 11.15, 11.16, and 11.17 on pages 148-150 for the proper procedure.)

I Saw Three Ships